WRITINGS FROM PRISON

D1617409

Writings from Prison

By

Leyla Zana

Forewords by

Elena Bonner & Betty Williams

Texts translated from Kurdish and Turkish by Kendal Nezan,
from French by Harriet Lutzky

BLUE CRANE BOOKS
WATERTOWN, MASSACHUSETTS

WRITINGS FROM PRISON
BY LEYLA ZANA

Published in 1999 by
Blue Crane Books
P.O.Box 291, Cambridge, MA 02238

Leyla Zana's writings were first published in French as
Écrits de prison by Des femmes, 1995.
This collection first published in English by Blue Crane Books, 1999.

First Edition
1   3   5   7   9   10   8   6   4   2

Cover design by Aramais Andonian
Photograph of Leyla Zana Courtesy of Istitut Kurde de Paris
Book design, typography & electronic pagination by
Arrow Graphics, Inc. Watertown, Massachusetts
Printed in Canada

Library of Congress Cataloging-in-Publication Data
Zana, Leyla, 1961–
[Ecrits de prison. English]
Writings from prison / Leyla Zana ; forewords by Elena Bonner
and Betty Williams. — 1st ed.
p.   cm. — (Human rights & democracy)
ISBN 1-886434-08-5 (alk. paper)
1. Zana, Leyla, 1961– —Correspondence.
2. Human rights—Turkey.
3. Kurds—Civil rights—Turkey.
4. Women political prisoners—Turkey—Correspondence.
I. Title. III. Series.
JC599.T87 Z3613   1999
323.1'1915970561—dc21   99-11873
CIP

CONTENTS

Acknowledgement

Special thanks to the directors and staff of Institut Kurde de Paris,
Dr. Harriet Lutzky, Washington Kurdish Institute, and Amnesty International
Somerville, Massachusetts Chapter for their invaluable editorial and research assistance.

Foreword

by

Elena Bonner

I think a book about a remarkable woman by the name of Leyla Zana needs no introduction. The life reflected on these pages speaks volumes and certainly a lot more than can be said by an author of any Foreword, however superlative. Indeed, Leyla Zana can truly be called a daughter of the Kurdish people, to whose rights she has devoted her life. She can also rightfully be called a self-made woman.

Leyla Zana was born in 1961, in a small Kurdish village. As a teenager, she was married to a man many years her senior who was actively involved in the Kurdish movement for national liberation and who introduced her to political activity. She was fifteen when she gave birth to a son, and soon after she became the first young woman in her town to be awarded a high school equivalency diploma. When Leyla was twenty, her husband, then the mayor of the town of Diyarbakir, was arrested and sentenced to thirty-years' imprisonment. At the time, Leyla was pregnant, and soon their daughter was born. A young mother with two small children destined to grow up fatherless, she continued her education, worked to create women's groups in Diyarbakir and Istanbul, and wrote for a newspaper.

In 1991 Leyla Zana became the first Kurdish woman to be elected to the Turkish Parliament, where she was one of the representatives of the sixteen million Turkish Kurds and worked to protect their rights. One has to keep in mind that for the Turkish Government no means are too low for the persecution of the Kurdish people, from bombarding Kurdish settlements and a scorched-land policy to prohibiting the use of their mother tongue.

The Turkish Government went so far as to change the green color of the traffic light to blue in Turkish Kurdistan because the Kurdish flag is a red-yellow-green tricolor.

In March 1994, Ms. Zana, together with three other Kurdish MPs, was stripped of their Parliamentary immunity, arrested, and, in December of that year, sentenced to fifteen years imprisonment. Her children were now left to the care of relatives and friends, while their mother became a symbol of the struggle against the genocide of the Kurdish people. Her uncompromising stand for human rights earned her the recognition of various international organizations, and she received many awards. Among them was the Sakharov Prize for Freedom of Thought awarded to Leyla Zana in 1996 by the European Parliament. While writing the nomination of Leyla for that prize, I kept thinking of the high price in freedom and even life paid by those who devote themselves to the struggle for human rights.

In the fall of 1997, I, too, was thinking of Leyla's plight, of the plight of her husband and children, and of their entire family. Together with my son's family, I was on my way to the lawn near the U.S. Capitol to greet a group of Kurdish activists and Kathryn Porter, the wife of U.S. Representative John Porter, who were holding a hunger strike to demand freedom for Leyla Zana. They stayed outside all day, spending the night in a nearby church. The day was gray and blustery cold, with a strong gusty wind, the kind that chills to the bone. We shook the hands of the fasting people.Their hands were very cold and their faces had a bluish hue. I realized that while no words of ours could warm them up, they were being kept warm, despite the cold hands and pale faces, by the hope that their voices would be heard.

This collective hunger strike lasted quite a while, and I wrote about it to the First Lady:

Dear Mrs. Clinton,

It is now twenty-nine days since the beginning of the hunger strike by the people who are trying to alleviate the suffering of Leyla Zana, the prisoner of conscience and laureate of the European Parliament's André Sakharov Prize. Ms. Zana has not committed any crimes; but with her words, she has tried to defend the rights of her people to live on their ancestral lands and to speak their own language.

I know the nature of a hunger strike, not from novels but from personal experience. Twenty-nine days is a long time; such a strike threatens not only the health, but also the very life of the hunger strikers. Kathryn Cameron Porter is among them. She is the wife of Congressman John Porter, and I understand you know her personally.

On 17 November the hunger strike was moved from the Capitol to the square in front of the White House. It is so close to your residence that your assistants can easily walk to the site and get all details about the case of Leyla Zana, this young woman who is a mother of two children and also is an elected member of the Turkish Parliament. I will not recount her case here., but I implore you to show compassion and understanding and to use your moral authority to help those who are striving for the release of Leyla Zana.

With respect and hope,
Elena Bonner

I received no response to this letter. After a Congressional resolution in support of the demands of the hunger strike, it ended. However, today, a year and a half years later, Leyla Zana is still imprisoned.

In May 1994, on her daughter's birthday, Leyla wrote her daughter, Ruken: "I would so much like to be with you today, on your birthday. But don't worry, we have a long life before us. We will have many birthdays to celebrate together. I wish you a happy birthday and send you many hugs and kisses, my heart." How many more years must pass before the entire Zana family celebrates a birthday together? I hope that the reader of this book will think of what he or she can do personally to hasten the day of freedom for Leyla Zana.

Elena Bonner,
Widow of André Sakharov and founder of
André Sakharov Institute for Peace
February 1999

Foreword

by

Betty Williams

In a world filled with ills and conflict—When was it ever not thus?—there are always people who stand up and speak for the simple rights of all human beings simply to exist.

Leyla Zana is such a person. Her courage shines like a beacon of compassion and understanding. And we can all be grateful that, today, we have the technology and the communicative ability to share in her story.

Throughout the past twenty-three years I have dedicated myself to the hard work of peace, and especially to working for the rights of women and children. It is a much misunderstood word—*peace*. But in every language it means not just the absence of violence and denial of basic human rights, but the simple right to exist without conflict, to be allowed, under whatever one believes his or her Supreme Being to be, to love and be loved, to hold true to the belief that all human beings-indeed, all creation—deserve justice and compassion, and that we are all one human family.

In recent months the world has witnessed the coming of peace to my homeland—Northern Ireland. But few remember that it was the women of Northern Ireland —the wives, mothers and daughters of Northern Ireland—who stood and raised their voices against the senseless cycle of useless violence we saw in our streets and across the beautiful green land of our birth. That voice, raised in courage and determination, announced a gentle but firm commitment to change, to doing things differently, to exposing the insanity of war and all forms of violence. It could not be silenced then, and it will never be silenced so long as there are women of courage—women like Leyla Zana—who will stand and demand that their voice be heard.

We must all have the courage—men and women alike—to listen when such a voice is raised. But more important, we must have the courage to act, to work together as a human family to ensure that such a voice is not silenced, shall never be silenced. Certainly, no human being should be incarcerated for his or her political beliefs.

Some of us will be awarded a Nobel Peace Prize for raising our voices. But those millions of others who raise their voices and are not recognized—who may never even be known outside their small area of influence—must continue against all odds, against all traditions, against all forms of insanity that would crush them and see them silenced forever.

Leyla, we honor your brothers and sisters who in defending justice have already paid the ultimate price with their lives, for they used the technique of nonviolence, which is truly the weapon of the strong.

God bless you, Leyla Zana; you will always be in my prayers.

Betty Williams
Nobel Peace Laureate and Founder and President,
World Centers of Compassion for Children.
October 1998

Nominating Leyla Zana
for the Nobel Peace Prize

The Nobel Peace Prize Committee
Oslo, Norway

Dear Committee Members:

Over the past century, an intractable problem on the world stage has confounded those policy makers who have attempted to achieve its resolution. The twenty-eighth president of the United States, Woodrow Wilson, felt that this matter should be treated as a question of self-determination. Today, it is also viewed, as it must be, as a profound humanitarian crisis. I am referring, of course, to the plight of the Kurdish people.

This ancient people continues today to face extreme difficulties. Their land continues to be the setting for war and destruction that has lasted, now, for decades. This situation seems to center, ultimately, on the tension and debate over the rights of native cultures versus the authority of the nations of the region. Yasar Kemal, Turkey's most famous author, has suggested for his part that both racism and greed play major roles in perpetuating the status quo. Lord Eric Avebury, the chairman of the Parliamentary Human Rights Group, who has extensively visited this region of the globe, invokes a famous quote by Tacitus to describe the present situation: "They made it a desolation and called it peace." In my own visit to Turkey this month, I saw palpable evidence of the human misery generated by the policies of war.

Many brave Kurdish souls have made the ultimate sacrifice to leap into the realm called peace for the benefit of themselves and their loved ones. Leyla Zana is one such individual. She has become a symbol of the yearning of the Kurds for a state of peaceful coexistence with their neighbors. Because of a lifetime of advocating peaceful coexistence, however, she has been imprisoned and now is serving the fourth year of a fifteen year sentence in Ankara Prison. At my initiation, 153 members of Congress signed a letter to President Clinton asking that he raise Leyla Zana's case with Turkish officials and that he seek to secure her immediate release from prison. In December of 1997, Amnesty International declared her a prisoner of conscience. In numerous European cities, she has been awarded honorary friendship and peace prizes.

I met with Leyla Zana in the course of my visit to Turkey. I met with members of the fledgling human rights communities in Istanbul and Ankara. I also spoke with government officials. I heard long and painful recriminations, but I also heard a deep longing for peace. It is plain that the Turks and the Kurds must talk to one another.

I am, accordingly, asking that you give your utmost consideration to the nomination of Leyla Zana for the 1998 Nobel Peace Prize, an act that could pave the way for the initiation of a dialogue that could bring peace. Such an award would symbolize both the hope for peace in the region and the degree to which the world is troubled by the lack of such peace. Such courageous action by the committee would serve to light a candle in a part of the world that has been kept in the darkness for too long. I hope you will agree that such a light is needed to bring an end to the long misery of the Kurds.

Sincerely,

John Edward Porter
Member of Congress
January 23, 1998

Among many other people who also nominated Leyla Zana for 1998 Nobel Peace Prize are John Austin, MP, House of Commons, England, Maartje Van Putten, Member European Parliament; and members of the U.S. Congress: Ken Calvert, Elizabeth Furse, Benjamin A. Gilman, Bob Filner, and Nick Lampson.

Letter from French President François Mitterrand

Madame Leyla Zana,
Member of Parliament

Dear Madam:

I have received your letter of 9 February sent to me by your lawyers through diplomatic channels, in which you describe to me your present situation and that of the parliamentarians imprisoned with you.

I was glad to learn that the reasons for the verdict against you have been made public. This will enable you to lodge an appeal with the Court of Appeals. I hope that your case will be dealt with in the same spirit of conciliation as that which prevailed in the recent acquittal of the presidents of the Turkish Foundation for Human Rights and the Turkish Association for Human Rights.

Let me assure you that France and the other states of the European Union, of which my country currently holds the presidency, will continue to take a close interest in your situation, as they have promised to do. Moreover, since the 8 December verdict and the immediate approach to the Turkish government made by the "troika of Ministers,"[1] representations on your behalf have been maintained. The 6 March meeting of the Council of Association with Turkey, in which the Customs Union Treaty was signed, gave us an opportunity to reiterate our concern.

I think that the signing of the Customs Union Treaty between Turkey and the European Union is a good thing. In fact, I am convinced, as are my European counterparts, that involving your country in Europe will promote democracy and encourage political and economic stability in Turkey. Turkey now seems well aware that its European aspirations imply the speedy adoption of concrete measures designed to promote democracy and respect for human rights and civil liberties. This is in fact the condition set by the European Parliament for endorsing the Customs Union Treaty. Your liberation and that of your fellow parliamentarians are among the concrete measures looked for from the Turkish government.

I trust that these possibilities will strengthen your courage and hope. Be assured that my country, as well as the other member states of the European Union, will continue to work for the swiftest possible end to your imprisonment, and for the establishment of a just state in Turkey.

With all my sympathy and sincere personal good wishes.

Yours faithfully,

François Mitterrand

Paris, April 24, 1995

1. The European Union's past, current, and future Foreign Affairs Ministers.

Preface to the French Edition

Claudia Roth
President of the European Parliament Greens Group

Dear Leyla:

I write this Preface to your book in the hope that one day, in the near future, you will be writing another book, in a place other than prison, a book that tells of a Kurdistan at peace.

I write this Preface in the hope that the journey you describe here—one of suffering, mourning, pain, and anger, one of courage and pride despite the hatred on the part of the state and the humiliation it subjects you to—may one day come to an end in a country without torture or tanks, where the thousands of destroyed villages will be rebuilt, and all who were sent into exile will return.

I write this Preface, Leyla, because you taught me what courage and strength are: "I love life, but my desire for justice is stronger" is what you told me. You were the first woman to make me understand (because you are a living example) what it means to have no rights.

You know, in the European Parliament, and especially among the Greens, we talk a lot about human rights and civil rights—but it was in talking to you that I first really came to understand what the lack of an independent civil justice system means, the extent to which police provocation and a ban on travel can change one's life, and what it means to be in constant fear that they might come "looking for" you, and that you might simply "disappear."

They came "looking for" Vedat Aydin—a few days later he was found buried in a ditch near Diyarbakir, beaten to death. His crime: he was a courageous man, a man of the Kurdish opposition, an ardent defender of human rights, someone who called crimes against humanity by their true name. It cost him his life. And it was at his funeral, the funeral of this friend who was a remarkable political analyst, full of projects and of a vision of the future for his country, that I met you for the first time, Leyla. At that moment, I saw something I had never seen before: a funeral attended by 100,000 people paying final homage to their martyr, where soldiers opened fire on the mourning crowd, beat members of Parliament, and finished off the wounded. Later, I was able to visit the seriously wounded in the hospital by going in through the back door. I saw a despairing Kurdish family around the bed of their fifteen-year-old son, their only source of support, crippled by a savage beating by the Turkish soldiers. I saw them forbid the hospital personnel to give blood to their compatriots. After that, I ended up in the editorial room of *Ulke*, a little newspaper that was banned a long time ago—and there I saw you, seated behind a desk, covered with bruises and bleeding everywhere, from the head, arms, and legs, because they had beaten you almost to death with staves. You were twenty years old, beautiful despite your black-and-blue marks and wounds. You smiled at me and told me about Vedat Aydin's funeral, of his fate, typical in a country that incarnates state terror and dirty warfare.

I was irritated, Leyla, and asked how anyone could keep working, go on surviving, while the best were being killed off. . . . In a combative tone, you answered: "For every man, for every women killed, others rise up and will continue to rise up." You never spoke of your own health, not then, not today, not even in prison in Ankara. Only once, you told me: "Some things are more important."

That is how our friendship began, with the help of our interpreter and friend Omer. But I felt I could understand you even without an interpreter. I gave you a sticker, a miniature representation of a poster that the Greens had designed based on something Danielle Mitterrand said: "Do not forget them. Silence kills." And also: "The Kurds, a forgotten people." Today that poster, with the Kurdish colors, is on a wall in my office. Perhaps it made you realize that you have many friends in Europe.

Since then, since the day of Vedat Aydin's funeral in Diyarbakir in the summer of 1990, we have seen each other often. How happy we were when you were elected member of the Turkish Parliament, when you were able to take your place alongside the other Kurdish members of the Party! We thought that the foundation was being laid for a political solution to the Kurdish question, but you were skeptical and remained so. How could it be otherwise when Kurdish women continued to be persecuted simply for braiding a ribbon with the Kurdish colors into their hair? You showed me how consistent and tenacious the women were in resisting. They wore the Kurdish colors—green-yellow-red—much more often than the men. And when I asked you if you were not being too much of a skeptic, you told me the story of the donkey. One day, in your region, the Turkish police arrested a donkey because he wore a bridle with the Kurdish colors. The police probably thought that the donkey would lead them to the "separatists." But, you told me laughing, in Kurdistan even the donkeys are not that dumb.

You told me many stories of this kind when you came to Strasbourg, Brussels, London, Paris, and New York, where you went to tell the world's politicians about what is really going on in the Kurdish regions. But the smile that the story elicits freezes when you know what happens to so-called separatists—prison, horrifying torture, peremptory execution. . . . Even Hell could not be worse.

And how easy it is to call a Kurd a "separatist!" Your husband, Mehdi, was sentenced to four years in prison because of a speech he made in the European Parliament. He had been invited by all the members of the Subcommission on Human Rights, who held their breath when he spoke of the situation in his country. He, the former mayor of Diyarbakir, after having spent eleven years in prison, had just been released in 1991. During the summer of 1994 he was back behind bars, two years for his speech to the European Parliament, and two more for giving reporters the text. There was nothing shocking in his talk, nothing but rights that are stipulated in human rights conventions and U.N. treaties, and that have become standard. He demanded nothing more than that the Kurds be able to enjoy their rights—to speak their own language, to sing their own songs, to live by their own customs and traditions. For this, your husband is in prison again—and in the European Parliament, we could do nothing to prevent this scandal. We could only register the facts, in anger and indignation.

During the summer of 1994, your family was definitively broken up—your husband thrown in prison, you stripped of your parliamentary immunity shortly beforehand, arrested right in Parliament and held in Ankara in preventive detention. I remember your invitation to come and see you the year before. Your house was full of friends and relatives, and you had prepared a Kurdish feast. That day I met your children, who now live far from you in Paris, far from their mother, far from their father, far from their country.

In the spring of 1994, after you and your collegues had been arrested, I was not permitted to come and visit you. Even though I had come to Turkey as a European Parliament observer of the local elections, I was not allowed to see you. I was also there at the opening of the so-called trial for high treason, that political trial in which you were the defendants. I was seated in the front row, and had only to stretch out my hand to touch you, but we were separated by soldiers armed to the teeth. You were guarded like big-time criminals. It was only that evening, on television, that I could see your face directly. How often did I try to visit you during that trial? I never got permission, certainly not after the public prosecutor Nusret Demiral demanded the death penalty, rudely insulting you and your friends, saying he had more respect for his dog than for you. I was furious to see so much contempt and cynicism.

In December 1994, you were sentenced to fifteen years in prison. At the time, I was attending a summit meeting of European heads of state. I listened to the news every half hour, and that is how I heard of your sentence after a trial in which nothing was legal.

Finally, in January 1995, I got the right to visit you. You had lost weight, but you remained positive and infinitely strong. You refused to talk about prison conditions. "Not worse than for the others," you said. We talked about women's role.

That role, you discovered, is oppressive and tragic, but the struggle to change it gives so many women, and men as well, the courage to continue to fight for a just life in peace and freedom.

I want to see you again where you belong—in Parliament. And I have a dream in which I hear you give a speech to the European Parliament, after which the Turkish ambassador leaps from his seat to shake your hand enthusiastically, saying: "How lucky there are women like you!"

Yours,

Claudia

October 1995

About Leyla Zana

Leyal Zana was born in 1961 to a traditional family in the small village of Bache in Eastern Turkey. One of four sisters and one brother, Leyla was a rebel from childhood. Defiant of the strict religion and a male dominated social order, she refused to wear a head scarf before she was married, and afterwords she wore one for a short time only.

She attended elementary school for a year and a half, only to be stopped by her extremely traditional father, who did not believe in educating girls.

At the age of fifteen she was married to her father's cousin, Mehdi Zana, a man twenty years her senior. Recalling her frustration at the time, when she angrily beat her father with her fists—something no other Kurdish girl would do—she says: "I don't blame my family or my husband, rather I blame the social conditions [in Kurdistan]. These must change."

Ironically, it was her marriage to Mehdi, a Kurdish activist, that presented her with the possibilities for change in both her personal and social conditions. Through him, Leyla encountered state repression in its fullest, and that inevitably politicized her.

After moving to Diyarbakir (the major Kurdish city in Eastern Turkey) with her husband, Leyla gave birth to their son, Ronay, in 1976. The following year, her husband was elected Mayor of Diyarbakir by an overwhelming margin.

The 1980 military coup in Turkey, however, brought about a new wave of oppression and persecution for Kurds. Political and individual freedoms were curtailed in the name of national security and democracy. Mehdi Zana was among thousands of activists who were arrested and tortured for their political beliefs. He was subsequently sentenced to thirty years in prison.

Leyla was now a young, single mother; her son, Ronay, was five, and she was pregnant with her daughter, Ruken. Whereas before she had been heavily influenced by her relatives, now she was forced, as she puts it, "to think for myself and act for myself." During the next few years, she followed her husband from prison to prison, from Diyarbakir to Aydin, from Afyon to Eskisehir. In the process, she learned to speak Turkish. Encouraged by her husband, she managed to study on her own and became the first woman in Diyarbaki, to receive a high school diploma without attending school.

As the number of prisoners grew, Leyla became more and more involved in the plight of women whose husbands were abducted and imprisoned by the military regime. Eventually, she became their spokesperson and assumed an unsolicited leadership role. In the 1980s, she was active in promoting women's rights and founded and chaired a women's group, which eventually opened offices in Istanbul and Diyarbakir. She worked for the Diyarbakir branch of the Human Rights Association and was a correspondent for *Yeni Ulke*, later taking on the editorial position at the paper's Diyarbakir office. In 1988 she was herself severely tortured; she still bears the physical and psychological scars. Her personal development was virtually synonymous with the development of the Kurdish liberation struggle, and this culminated in her candidacy for Parliament in the 1991 elections in Turkey.

In October 1991, Leyla Zana was the first Kurdish woman to be elected to the Turkish Parliament. An extremely popular candidate, she received 84 percent of the votes in her district in Diyarbakir. An advocate of peace and of an end to the civil war raging in southeast Turkey, Leyla protested vehemently against the violence perpetrated by the Turkish Government toward the 16 million Kurds in Turkey.

On 17 May 1993 she was invited to Washington, D.C., together with Ahmet Turk, another Kurdish parliamentarian, to brief members of the U.S. Congress at the Helsinki Commission and to speak at the Carnegie Endowment for International Peace. She spoke of the destruction of Kurdish villages and the Kurdish people, and of the inability of the Turkish and Kurdish political leaders to address the Kurdish question with frankness and candor. She urged the U.S. Congress to side with the democratic forces in Turkey and to help bring about a peaceful resolution to the Kurdish conflict. Little did she know that her Washington talks would be used against her in the State Security Court in Ankara.

In March 1994 Leyla Zana and her colleagues Hatip Dicle, Orhan Dogan, Selim Sadak (in July), all Kurdish members of the Parliament, were stripped of their Parliamentary immunity and arrested. Charges of separatism and illegal activities were brought against the four for publicly advocating peaceful coexistence between the Turkish and Kurdish peoples. Expression of Kurdish identity in Parliament and even the color of their clothes were used as evidence against them. "That the defendant Leyla Zana on 18 October 1991 did wear clothes and accessories in yellow, green, red [colors associated with Kurdish flag] while addressing the people of Cizre on 18 October 1991." This statement was part of the grounds cited in convicting Leyla Zana (Verdict of Ankara State Security Court No 1, page 555). (See Appendix A: The Color of Their Clothes.)

In December 1994, the panel of Turkish civil and military judges convicted all four Parliamentarians. Leyla was sentenced to fifteen years in prison.

Since her arrest, a tremendous effort has been launched on her behalf by human rights organizations and the diplomatic community worldwide. She has received international recognition and numerous peace awards, among them the Raftos Prize for Human Rights from Norway (1994); the Bruno Kreisky Peace Prize from Austria (1995); the Aix-la-Chapelle International Peace Prize from Germany (1995); the Rose Prize from Denmark (1996); and the Sakharov Prize for Freedom of Thought from the European Parliament (1995). In 1995, she was nominated for the Nobel Peace Prize for the first time and was a finalist. She was nominated for the Nobel Peace Prize for the third time in 1998 by, among others, U.S. Representative John Porter, Democrat of Illinois.

In April 1998, The Val d'Aosta Regional Council (Northern Italy) awarded its Woman of the Year Prize to Leyla Zana.

François Stevenin, President of the Council, praised Leyla for her dedication: "First Kurdish woman in Turkish history to be elected to Parliament, she has sacrificed one's most fundamental possession, freedom, to defend her people. Sentenced and jailed in Ankara Prison, she has become the symbol of Kurdish struggle for the recognition of democratic values based on peace and social justice."

In an interview published in the 13 August 1998 issue of the Turkish daily *Milliyet,* Leyla is unwavering in her beliefs. "So long as the Turkish Constitution of 1982 remains in force, I cannot believe there will be any real improvement or democratization [in Turkey]," she said. "I do not personally expect to be freed. . . . At one time the question of my release was raised, though for the wrong reasons. . . . What difference would my release make? Turkey's problems, the war, torture would all remain. Only I would be outside. Why? Outside to serve as a bit of window dressing for European public opinion. But I do not want to serve as decoration. For a while I was not well. The state decided that I was seriously ill so as to be able to release me on those grounds without admitting its errors. Today I feel better. The state continues to inflict new prison sentences on us and will go on doing so as long as we go on speaking and writing. Let them. I submit. My husband, my daughter, and my son are all out of the country. I remain here alone, but I accept my situation."

On 26 September 1998, on the very day that the European Parliament launched another appeal to the Turkish authorities for the immediate release of Leyla Zana, the Ankara State Security Court sentenced her to another two years in jail for an article that had appeared in the People's Democracy Party (HADEP) bulletin about *Nevruz,* the Kurdish New Year. According to the Court, by writing about the distinct identity of the Kurds, their ancestral traditions, and their struggle against oppression and for freedom, Ms. Zana has committed the crime of "inciting race hatred." [See the full text of this article on page 88]

In the past year, prison conditions have worsened for the Kurdish M.P.'s. Visitors are banned, and even the immediate family is not allowed the privilege of a private room. Medical care has become more difficult and is accompanied by various forms of harassment, insults, and ill-treatment. Leyla Zana, who is now suffering from a liver condition in addition to her advanced osteoporosis, refuses hospital visits under military escort, in protest against the maltreatment of political prisoners in Turkey. Meanwhile, the proceedings before the European Court for Human Rights on the petition for the release of the Kurdish M.P.'s is moving very slowly. It is unlikely that any verdict will be reached before the end of 1999.

Leyla Zana's husband, son, and daughter are in exile, and in spite of all international protest, she remains in Ankara Central Prison at the time of this publication.

Speaking Out

Shut up, woman!

What woman has never heard that order from a husband, father, or brother, personifying domestic power? In a meeting of my party's parliamentary group, one member of Parliament, known as a democrat and a progressive, cut me off, saying I should let the men speak first, as in our good old patriarchal tradition! I was dumbstruck. I had to explain, calmly, that I had been elected with nearly twice the number of votes he had, that the voters had chosen me so that I would speak out and express their suffering and their wishes in Parliament, in the media, and before an international audience, and that furthermore, I had as much right to speak as anyone else.

He apologized for his attitude, the effect of age-old habits, and no one in my party has ever again dared interrupt me or claim male privilege. The tendency was even reversed. My colleagues always wanted me to be first to express myself, which I also refused. I wanted to be considered a human being in my own right, to express myself on an equal basis with men. It took time for my friends in the party to put the concept of equality into practice, but they finally got used to it.

In Parliament, there were only 8 women out of 450 members, and I was the only Kurdish woman. Attempts to engage my Turkish women colleagues in dialogue were unsuccessful, probably because of nationalist prejudice. Also, I think each was the protégée of some clique or faction, and they feared for their careers. For fear of displeasing the powerful men, they almost never spoke and were content to be bit players.

The first time I spoke in Parliament was when I took the oath of office. I had to swear on the Constitution, solemnly swear to respect the principles of that antidemocratic document, written and imposed by the 1980 military junta. It was all the more painful because the Constitution legitimizes a particularly repressive military coup d'état that established Turkish nationalism and Atatürk's no-less nationalist principles as official state ideology. It codified into law the negation of the Kurdish people and criminalized any affirmation of Kurdish identity. In sum, the Turkish political-military establishment asked us, the elected representatives of the Kurdish people, to publicly renounce our identity, the raison d'être of our democratic struggle, and to pledge our allegiance to its system. Without that public, televised act of allegiance, our mandates as members of Parliament would not be validated.

How could we avoid the trap set for us from the very outset of our parliamentary careers? Everyone, particularly the people who elected us, waited to see what the "Pasionaria of the Kurds" (as the press had dubbed me), would do. I felt the pressure of overwhelming responsibility. I was determined not to give in and, to emphasize my commitment to my identity, wore a scarf with Kurdish colors. When my name was called, a heavy silence fell in the packed hall of Parliament. The distance separating my seat from the podium seemed endless. When I reached the podium I saw an imposing group of decorated generals in the gallery, as well as a number of foreign diplomats. The party chairmen and all the members of the government attended the ceremony, which was transmitted live on television. This was my hour of truth, I said to myself. The little Kurdish peasant girl thrown into the lion's den.

I mustered all my strength to cope with the situation. First, I calmly read the Turkish text of the oath, which formally validated my mandate. Then, I added the following sentence in Kurdish and also in Turkish: "I underwent that formality under duress. I will fight for the fraternal coexistence of the Kurdish and Turkish peoples within the context of democracy."

Those few words set off a scene of collective hysteria in the hall. Cries of "Separatist! Traitor!" were heard from all sides. Prime Minister Süleyman Demirel, usually placid, was one of the most furious. I thought he was going to have apoplexy. Some members of Parliament shouted: "Arrest her! Hang her!"

The extraordinary power of language! It took only a few words, rather banal at that, but spoken in a banned language (an incomprehensible tongue, according to the minutes of the session) to infuriate this fine company—educated, civilized and considering themselves democrats. True, it was the first time in the history of the Turkish Republic that anyone dared pronounce a Kurdish sentence in Parliament. And it had to be a woman who made this iconoclastic gesture.

At that point, the die was cast. The Turkish establishment considered me beyond redemption, an enemy to be defeated. The president of the party I belonged to at the time—the Social Democrat Populist Party [SHP]—Mr. Erdal Inönü, son of a former president of the Republic, physics professor and Western-educated polyglot, later to become vice-president of the Socialist International, demanded my resignation and that of my colleague from Diyarbakir, Hatip Dicle, who had also objected to the military-inspired Turkish Constitution.

We refused to comply with his order, leaving the party the choice of whether or not to expel us for our opinions. But a little more than a year later, after the army massacred a hundred Kurdish civilians while crushing a Kurdish New Year's demonstration at Cizre on 21 March, 1992, I and about twenty other Kurdish members of Parliament resigned because of the inaction of the leadership of the SHP, which was a member of the government coalition. We regrouped and formed our own party, the People's Labor Party [HEP].

I was virtually forbidden to take the floor in Parliament, where I was feeling more and more alienated. The government-controlled media and political police portrayed me as a "separatist" and refused to publish my statements, or published only distorted passages for their shock value. I therefore decided to get out of that ghetto, to break the wall of silence and disinformation surrounding the tragedy of my people by making my voice heard abroad, speaking to Western media and leaders. Like a press attaché, I brought reporters and delegations of foreign observers to the sites of destroyed Kurdish villages and to visit tormented families.

In a region whose fate has been left to the discretion of the army and its auxiliary militia,[1] and where death squads assassinated Kurdish democrats, members of Parliament with their parliamentary immunity were the only ones able to bear witness, which disturbed the military greatly. I became their bête noire. The police and special army units used my photo in target practice to personify the enemy to defeat. After many verbal threats, underscored by the assassination of about sixty of our party's leaders and activists, the army decided to strike at the top by directly attacking the members of Parliament.

Obviously, I was at the head of their blacklist. A commando was to kill me and my colleague Mehmet Sincar, member of Parliament from Mardin, during our parliamentary delegation's trip to Batman to attend the funeral of the president of the party's departmental federation who had just been assassinated by a death squad. During the funeral, the police were responsible for protecting us. But after the ceremony, they withdrew their protection, even though they knew we were going to visit shopkeepers in the city. Worn out with fatigue and pain due to my poor health, I was not able to take part in the trip to the city during which, on 4 September 1993 a commando shot Mehmet Sincar point blank, killing him and wounding another member of Parliament, Nizamettin Toguç, who had accompanied him.

A few days later, during Mehmet Sincar's funeral, there was another attempt on my life. The house I was staying in was sprayed with machine gun fire. By pure chance I was in another room watching the late news on television, and once again escaped death. I must surely have *baraka*.[2]

How can a nation, one of the oldest on earth, with an army of 800,000 soldiers and considerable police and militia force, and with an imposing diplomatic and media corps, be afraid of a few citizens who have, as their only weapon, the power of speech? Why this relentlessness against peaceful democrats whose only missions are to improve the lot of their people and to establish friendly and mutually respectful relations with their Turkish neighbors?

The great Kurdish film maker and thinker Yilmaz Güney was surely right in saying that sometimes a word, an image, or a song can be the most dreaded weapon, like the grain of sand that can jam the most sophisticated machine.

Certainly a totalitarian ideology, based on lies, fears words of truth that, like tiny viruses, can threaten its apparently solid and imposing edifice.

In spite of the attempts on my life and the daily threats made against me and my family, I was determined not to give in, but rather to go abroad to talk about the fate of my people. After a visit to the United States at the invitation of a U.S. Congressional Commission,[3] and a series of meetings in the Scandinavian countries and in England and Germany, our party decided to organize a diplomatic tour to explain both the tragedy of our people and the situation of our members of Parliament threatened with loss of parliamentary immunity, arrest, and the death penalty.

This delegation, composed of the members of Parliament Ahmet Türk, Sirri Sakik, Orhan Dogan, and myself, was received on 4 February 1994 in Paris at the Elysée Palace by President François Mitterrand, in Strasbourg by Catherine Lalumière, Secretary General of the Council of Europe, and in Brussels by Jacques Delors, president of the European Commission; they all received us with respect and listened attentively as we presented our case. The press gave wide coverage to these high-level contacts, which were the beginning of the internationalization of the Kurdish problem in Turkey.

Back in Turkey to talk things over with our colleagues and plan the rest of our tour of Western countries, we were met with the strongarm tactics of a government panicked by our international audience. Called to an emergency plenary session just two days before the break to prepare for municipal elections, the Turkish Parliament, surrounded by police and the army, voted posthaste to lift the immunity of all members of Parliament who took part in our diplomatic delegation, as well as of two other potential "diplomatic" members of Parliament. This shameful vote took place in the absence of the president of the Parliament and the chairpersons of the major parties, except for Mrs. Çiller. The question of lifting immunity, the one-hundred-fifty-first item on the Parliament's agenda, had thus been advanced and hastily dealt with in a climate of coup d'état, under military threat. We were arrested and thrown into prison.

They thus wanted, once again, to silence us. A strong international reaction prevented the government from dispersing us to the far corners of the provinces and forced it to keep us together in Ankara and to permit regular visits from our lawyers and families.

Thus, we went from the big, open-air prison that Turkey is today for the Kurds and for Turkish democrats to being shut up within four walls, behind bars, for many years.[4] I had always said that even if they shut me up in a fortress or chained my body, they could not shackle my spirit. With my last breath I would continue to speak out, write and declare my message of peace, brotherhood, and democracy. From the depths of my prison, I have continued to write, send letters to Western political leaders, do articles for newspapers, and send messages of thanks and solidarity to all those who support the struggle of my people for the respect of its dignity and identity. Like bottles thrown into the sea, some of these messages have been lost en route, seized by Turkish jailers and censors. Others have reached their destination, and they are the basis of this writing from prison.

Naturally, this writing is not a structured work. It is made up of fragments of life, emotion, and reaction, and notes of my thoughts, set down at the request of my friend Antoinette Fouque[5] whose presence at several of my trial hearings and whose letters of support have touched me greatly. This is my modest contribution to the cause of women that she has long advocated with such energy and devotion.

But the world would be an unlivable place without its masculine half. Even though we have much to reproach men for, we could not do without them. We cannot build a better and more just world without them nor against them, but only with them, educating them and helping them overcome sexist prejudices if need be, in day-to-day struggle, endlessly renewed. Nor are they all macho—far from it. The publication of this collection owes a great deal to the constant encouragement of one of those progressive men, my friend of long standing, Kendal Nezan,[6] who has done so much for the advancement of Kurdish women.

With this collection I would like to send Kurdish women, and all other women as well, the same message of struggle: Speak out! Take the floor! Express yourself in every way! No one should every again say to us, "Shut up, woman!" Let us refuse to be silent! Speaking freely is a decisive step forward on the road to freedom.

25 May 1995

1. Martial law and emergency rules suspend Constitutional guarantees and give all power to a governor or army commander.
2. "I must surely be blessed."
3. The Commission on Security and Cooperation in Europe, referred to as the Helsinki Commission.
4. On 8 December 1994, Leyla Zana and four of her colleagues were sentenced to fifteen years in prison, and three others to sentences of from three-and-one-half to seven-and-one-half years in prison.
5. French Member of the European Parliament, president of the Women's Alliance for Democracy, and publisher of the French edition of this book.
6. Founder and president of the Kurdish Institute of Paris.

Let Us Defend Diversity

Toward the end of 1993, I went to Paris for treatment. Fourteen years of stress, barbaric torture suffered during my two months in custody in 1988, two recent attempts on my life, and innumerable death threats orchestrated by the Turkish secret services had gotten the better of my health. I was at the end of my rope, both physically and emotionally.

"You need a general checkup; you've probably overdone it; the machine isn't working any more," joked Kendal Nezan, my friend who is exiled in Paris.

In spite of the Kurdish political realities, which leave no time for rest, I felt I should accept his invitation. After the Democracy Party [DEP] Congress, held in Ankara with more than fifteen thousand delegates and guests, I took leave of my colleagues and went to Paris.

During my stay there, between two hospitalizations, my friend introduced me to men and women politicians and intellectuals and to French, American, and other journalists, so that I might broaden my horizons, increase my contacts, and be able to spread my message.

That is how I happened to lunch one day with some highly placed well-known French public figures. A bit intimidated despite the courtesy and kindness they showed me, I felt that they wanted to know how one could be a Kurd and why one would want to remain Kurdish.

After a moment one of the guests asked me: "Madam, you are Kurdish and it hasn't prevented you from becoming a member of Parliament. I think, by the way, that your Minister of Foreign Affairs is himself of Kurdish descent, and that there are several Kurdish ministers in the cabinet. What exactly do you want? Why do you refuse to become Turkish? Why do you want to speak and preserve your language?"

I have often heard that kind of question in Turkey, but to hear it in France, and from the mouth of an eminent socialist spirit, disconcerted me somewhat. Maybe he was just testing me, getting me to respond to a question that, after all, anyone might wonder about. Suddenly my friend's warning came to mind: "Don't forget that France is the country of radicalism and assimilation. The French steamroller has eliminated local languages and culture in France and, on the pretext of universality, has set a very bad example for the nationalist and assimilationist regimes of other countries.

Raised in the countryside, loving nature and the extraordinary diversity that gives it its richness and magic, I was not going to launch into theoretical and political explanations.

"The relation to language is vital, essential. It is an almost physical love. Nothing in the world could get us to give up our mother tongue. Look—every bird likes to sing in its own way. The rose is without a doubt a very beautiful flower. Yet a flower bed made up only of roses would be monotonous and boring, while a garden where a thousand and one varieties of flowers bloom is a real pleasure to look at, an inexhaustible source of inspiration and beauty. In the garden of languages, Kurdish may not be a rose claiming universality, nor a stylish orchid, nor a royal lily. It is only a modest snowdrop, poppy, or wild flower. But these flowers have the right to live, too, and they make poets and lovers happy. Life also means the right of the weak, the unnecessary, and the marginal to exist," I answered with a passion that amazed me later on.

I also added that the presence of ministers who, though of Kurdish descent, completely deny their identity and are greater Turkish nationalists than the Turks themselves does not at all prove that the Kurds have been well treated in Turkey. For the Kurdish people affirm their identity, and even when they peacefully seek rights for their community, they are systematically hunted and persecuted. Even Saddam Hussein, who massacred the Kurds by the tens of thousands, always had a few servile ministers of Kurdish descent in his government. The Janissaries, the Ottoman Empire's shock troops, were all of non-Turkish descent and were used by the Sultan to suppress the liberation movements of their own peoples violently. That the Kurds of Turkey also have a few Janissary ministers does not at all affect their fate.

As for the question of assimilation, I wonder why Western democrats do not understand the gravity of the issue. The disappearance of any language or culture, which is the fruit of the labor of generations of men and women over centuries, is an impoverishment, an irreparable mutilation of the world's heritage.

And then, where would such a philosophy lead us? Today, the disappearance of Kurdish in favor of Turkish or Arabic, of Quechua in favor of Spanish, of Basque or Breton in favor of French, seems acceptable. Tomorrow, we will feel that the minor European languages like Dutch, Swedish, Norwegian, Danish, or Hungarian have no reason to exist when faced with the major languages like German, English, Spanish, or French. Then, this chain of events will bring us to a sad, monotonous world, dominated by Anglo-Americans. Even our proud French friends will have to defend their identity and culture from Anglo-American domination.

By fiercely defending my language, my identity, and my culture, I do not have the feeling that I am defending something archaic, or a mere local oddity. On the contrary, I think I am contributing to the preservation of the universal, whose sap is nourished by diversity. Uniformity is the death of civilization. There is no universal without the living individual, solidly rooted in its own territory. Exalting the differences could lead to conflict, but trying to suppress them can, too. For me, true humanism is respect for the human community with its diversity of language and culture, and defining the rules and structures that will permit the development of each, just as we respect nature and the infinite diversity of species that makes for its richness and balance.

21 February 1995

For Taslima Nasrin

All I know of Taslima Nasrin's ideas come from the few things published in the Turkish press. Her challenge of the established order, her defense of the Bangladeshi Hindu minority, and her struggle against religious fundamentalism all appeal to me. Without ever having seen or heard her, I consider her a sister in struggle. We women have great need of courageous fighters like her, particularly in Islamic lands, where we still do not have a voice.

The fact that there are a few women ministers here and there, window dressing for authoritarian regimes, and even a woman prime minister, as in Bangladesh and Turkey, has not the least effect on our condition of servitude. In order to keep their positions, these ambitious women feel obliged to be even harder and more pitiless than their male colleagues. Our prime minister [Tansu Çiller] is a good example. Chosen by the Turkish politi-

---

Taslima Nasrin, a Bangladeshi doctor and writer, is an outspoken critic of the oppression of women in Moslem society. Outraged reactions to her 1993 novel *Shame* (which denounced Moslem violence against members of the Bangladeshi Hindu minority) and to a 1994 newspaper interview that quoted her as calling for a thorough revision of the Koran (though she has denied having said this, claiming that she had called for changes in the Sharia, Islamic law, in order to grant equal status to men and women) brought her worldwide attention. The Bangladeshi government, pressured by Islamic fundamentalist groups, charged Nasrin with blasphemy and put a warrant out for her arrest; this coupled with death threats against her and members of her family, prompted her to go into hiding. Support from several Western governments and also from International PEN Women Writers' Committee and Amnesty International enabled Nasrin to leave Bangladesh in 1994; she has been living abroad since then. Taslima Nasrin was awarded the European Parliament's Sakharov Prize for Freedom of Thought in 1994. Nasrin's books in English are *The Game in Reverse: Poems*, translated by Carolyne Wright, New York: George Brazillier, 1995, and *Shame: A Novel*, translated by Kankavati Datta, Prometheus Books, 1997. (From "The Perils of Free Speech: The Life and Writings of Taslima Nasrin," Carolyne Wright, *Organica,* Autumn 1995, pp. 18–20).

cal-military establishment for her charm and image of "modernity" (she has a degree from an American university), she has become a willing propagandist for a bellicose, warriorlike, militaristic policy. The generals consider her their best spokesperson, and she calls General Güres, Army Chief of Staff and true master of the country, "*abi*" (big brother) in public, and President [Süleyman] Demirel, "*baba*" (papa). Under the dual guardianship of "big brother" and "father," not to mention her husband, the woman claims to embody modernity and the emancipation of Turkish women.

What a caricature of women's struggle for equality! Woman's body is used to sell all sorts of consumer products. Here, the authoritarian regimes, seeking credit in the West, use women as political models to give themselves a modern, secular image. Within the country, this manipulation does disservice to the cause of women and confuses men and women who expect more humanism and more tolerance and democracy from the emergence of women into positions of power. I must admit that I was one of the first to be disappointed. When Mrs. Tansu Çiller was designated prime minister, I was happy and full of hope. I thought deep down inside that a woman, a mother, a person educated in the West and thus in principle steeped in the values of tolerance, democracy, and feminism, might bring a new spirit to outdated Turkish politics. Though I was a member of the parliamentary opposition, I did my best. I did not vote against her appointment.

After that experience, I realize that a few token women will not change women's situation, because they do not truly reflect the level of social consciousness of the public. They are there merely because of men's will, their power games, their seduction, and their foreign policy.

How can we raise people's consciousness in Moslem societies? If I have correctly understood Taslima Nasrin's thinking, as presented in the Turkish press, the fact that almost all the interpreters of the Koran have been men plays a role in the current status of Moslem women. Without a doubt. I do not know enough about this to see whether a feminine interpretation of the Koran is possible, or if it would succeed in transforming consciousness, or if the emancipation of Moslem women depends on a reinterpretation of the Koran. I merely note that in another monotheistic religion, Catholicism, despite centuries of effort at reform, interpretation and dialogue, the Pope can still condemn contraception and abortion and thus deny women the right to dispose of their bodies, lives, and sexuality. My feeling is that all monotheistic religions are based on male domination. The prophets, caliphs, apostles, popes, rabbis and ayatollahs are all men.

In our societies divided by religious and national differences, the true emancipation of women does not seem possible except in the framework of a pluralistic, secular democracy. Let us give believers freedom of conscience and create structures that guarantee that freedom without allowing anyone to impose his or her beliefs on others. In such a framework, our emancipation can be achieved only through education, culture, work, and a daily struggle against sexist discrimination. We must teach our children, brothers, husbands, and fathers that the development of each of us requires respect for the other, and the equality of the sexes. In Moslem societies shaped by centuries of patriarchal tradition, this struggle will be particularly difficult. The pioneers will suffer and have to put up with all kinds of insults and ordeals. By fighting for the emancipation of women, we will bring an essential contribution to the struggle for democracy. From Algeria to Bangladesh, by way of Kurdistan and Iran, women's struggle will be the main force of democratic resistance to fundamentalist barbarity.

16 November 1994.

Facing the Death Penalty in Ankara for My Beliefs

Turkey has a long tradition of political trials in which, after a military coup, politicians, even members of Parliament and ministers, are arrested, sentenced, and thrown into prison.

But even in this context, the proceedings against me and other Kurdish members of Parliament represent a new departure in the country's political life. This is the first time that under a reputedly civilian government, elected representatives have been imprisoned, brought to trial for their opinions, and threatened with capital punishment.

This trial is a purely political one. Even before we appeared in court, Prime Minister Tansu Çiller, several other ministers, and heads of Turkish political parties had publicly judged and condemned us. During the campaign for last year's municipal elections, Prime Minister Çiller claimed: "I threw the traitors out of Parliament." The government spokesperson branded us "terrorists," and the state television channels, in special programs, widely diffused government propaganda against us. In such a context, when even Parliament serves as nothing more than a rubber stamp, it is not possible to believe in the independence and impartiality of the Turkish justice system.

This justice system wants me condemned to death for the peaceful, legal activity I have carried out in my capacity as member of Parliament from Diyarbakir since October 1991. It

This article is an abstract of the defense presented by Leyla Zana on 5 August 1994 before the State Security Court of Ankara. On 5 September, the French daily *Libération* published almost the whole text, followed on 24 September by the Dutch daily *NRC Handelsblad*. Other European papers, notably *The Times* and *The Independent* of London, published long excerpts. These publications aroused angry reactions from the progovernment Turkish media. Ilnur Çevik, editor-in-chief of the *Turkish Daily News*, accused Leyla Zana in that paper (the most moderate one) "of not considering herself one of us," "of having no confidence in Turkish justice," and "of denouncing her country abroad."

reproaches me for opinions expressed in Parliament, in election meetings, and in the local and international press, as well as for going on a hunger strike to protest the army's destruction of the Kurdish city of Sirnak—all appeals for peace and dialogue.

My worst crime, in the view of the prosecution, seems to be a phrase I spoke in Kurdish on the brotherhood of Kurds and Turks and their coexistence in equality and democracy when I took the loyalty oath in Parliament. Even the color of my clothes seems to have been a "separatist crime." Furthermore, simply by mentioning the existence of the Kurdish people and Kurdistan, by peaceably demanding recognition of Kurdish culture and identity in a democratic system and within existing borders, I have supposedly defended the aims of the Kurdistan Workers' Party [PKK], which would make me "a member of the political wing of that party." But that party is engaged in armed struggle, while all my activity is aimed at silencing the weapons and seeking a peaceful solution to the Kurdish problem.

Nor am I alone in speaking of the existence of the Kurds. Our late president, Turgut Özal, spoke publicly of the "twelve million Kurds in Turkey" and openly discussed possible solutions, including a federal solution, to this chronic problem. The current president, Süleyman Demirel, declared in 1991 that "From now on, Turkey recognizes the Kurdish reality."

The Kurdish people are not the product of my imagination. Historians agree that the Kurds have inhabited their present land since time immemorial, and that they have a language, culture, and civilization of their own. Between 1806 and 1937, my people carried out no fewer than twenty-eight uprisings to gain their freedom. Although all were violently put down, they nonetheless show the historic depth of Kurdish national aspirations. President Demirel himself called the current guerrilla movement the "twenty-ninth uprising."

At the end of World War I, when a vanquished Turkey was threatened with being wiped off the map, the Kurds generously came to the aid "of the Turks in distress," supporting Mustafa Kemal and his friends, who promised to create a new state in which Kurds would obtain their full rights and seventy-five Kurdish notables would sit as "members of Parliament from Kurdistan" in Turkey's first Parliament. On 10 February 1922 Kemal presented a bill consisting of nineteen articles on the "Province of Kurdistan and its Parliament." However, study of the bill was delayed by various maneuvers until after the Treaty of Lausanne was signed in July 1923, recognizing the new Turkish state.

From then on, Kemal's first task was to pass a new Constitution based on Turkish nationalism and the negation of the Kurds in order to build a "Turkish nation-state." The Kurdish representatives and chiefs who had helped him in his war of independence were all sent to the gallows on various pretexts by the sadly renowned Independence Courts, forerunners of the current State Security Courts that judge us today. The 1924 Constitution forbade the use of Kurdish and any other language spoken in Turkey, except Turkish. Pseudotheories, proving "the Turkishness of the Kurds," were imposed on the country.

Since then, Turkey has pretended that there are no Kurds, but that the Kurds are "mountain Turks." Turkey has carried out an intense assimilation campaign, forcibly changing the ancient Kurdish names of our cities and villages into Turkish, and going so far as to forbid us from giving our children Kurdish names. Some Kurdish intellectuals have been bought off with jobs and payments, and those who refused to cooperate have been eliminated by heavy prison sentences or exile. This systematic policy was followed even after the formal transformation of the country to a multiparty system in 1950. The Kurdish elite was decimated. In 1971, a left wing Turkish party, the Turkish Labor Party [TIP], with representatives in Parliament, was disbanded for having recognized "the existence of the Kurdish people in Eastern Turkey."

The military coup of 12 September 1980 unleashed massive, violent repression on the country. In a country devoted to the universal values of democracy and liberty, the whole population would have descended into the streets to oppose the dictatorship. But Turkey, unfortunately, does not yet have such traditions. Today's serious crisis stems directly from that coup d'état, and from the abusive 1982 Constitution that it imposed by bayonet, the laws that destroyed liberty, and the institutions and political parties that all come out of the same mold, fashioned by the military dictatorship. It is therefore not surprising that all current

Turkish political parties accept the principles of a Constitution based on the negation of the Kurds and their rights.

This is the logic that permitted the Social Democrat Populist Party [SHP] of Mr. Erdal İnönü to expel seven of its members of Parliament for having attended (without even taking the floor) a Kurdish conference on human rights organized in October 1989 in Paris by the Fondation France-Libertés and the Kurdish Institute of Paris. That decision showed everyone that there was no true political pluralism in Turkey, and that it was time to create a new party. That is how the People's Labor Party [HEP] was founded in June 1990; and then, after it was banned, the Democracy Party [DEP] was founded, addressing both Kurds and Turks, and proposing to find a peaceful solution to the Kurdish problem in Turkey within the framework of democracy.

This was enough for the Turkish political establishment to call us "separatists" and even "terrorists." We have become the enemy to defeat, the favorite target of the Turkish counterguerrilla forces. In less than two years these forces have assassinated fifty-four of our leaders, including my colleague Mehmet Sincar, member of Parliament from Mardin. I myself barely escaped two attempts on my life.

Neither assassination nor death threats have silenced us. We have continued to work for dialogue between the country's Kurdish and Turkish communities and have continued to bear witness in Turkey and abroad to the tragedy of the Kurdish people brought on by army massacres and destruction of our cities and villages. It is because our voice has finally begun to be heard in Europe and the United States that the government has decided to silence us by lifting our parliamentary immunity, throwing us into prison, and banning the Democracy Party [DEP].

However, the government is mistaken if it thinks it will silence the Kurds by banning our party. This action clearly shows that democracy is nothing but a façade in Turkey. The way our immunity was lifted and we, the elected representatives of the people, were thrown into prison has seriously tarnished the regime's image in the West, where the belief is widespread that this has been done at the behest of the army. In fact, the banning of the DEP has internationalized Turkey's Kurdish problem even more.

Internally, the state hoped that by banning our party it could prevent the Kurdish struggle for freedom and democracy from developing on the legal and political levels.

In so doing, it has destroyed a prime instrument in the Kurdish-Turkish dialogue for a democratic solution to the Kurdish question in Turkey. The political parties, who were unable to seize the opportunity, the media which provide disinformation, the social and professional organizations that take refuge in silence, the intellectuals shirking their duty—all share responsibility for the bloody trial that is going on and for the serious losses suffered by our two peoples.

A political party has the right and the duty to express its opinions on the country's problems and to make these problems public. We have acted according to our convictions and to what we believe to be in the interest of the country and of democracy. We have worked to prevent more blood and tears and to find peaceful solutions to the country's serious problems.

We are essentially being reproached for having expressed our opinions (within a context of freedom of expression) on the coexistence of the Turks, Kurds, and other peoples of Turkey on a basis of true equality, liberty, and fraternity. We have not committed any violent acts, nor have we condoned violence. Our only "crime" is our resolute and firm attachment to our democratic and peaceful demands. Whatever the outcome of our trial, we will never renounce our beliefs or our demands. No one should doubt that we will defend these beliefs and demands whatever the cost, and that we will exert all our force toward a peaceful settlement of the Kurdish question, for that is our mandate.

If Galileo, despite the threat of the Inquisition, could still say "but it does move," then I can say that I will still struggle on behalf of the Kurdish people; their existence is a fact just as real as the movement of the earth.

As the first Kurdish women elected as member of Parliament, I risk being sentenced to death for my beliefs in support of peace, democracy, and the recognition of the legitimate rights of my people. And it is a state considered "democratic," a member of NATO and of the Council of Europe, benefiting in many ways from Western support, that, at the dawn of the twenty-first century, wants to burn me at the stake. Does this shock public opinion less than the condemnation of Taslima Nasrin by fundamentalist groups? Despairing of governments, who are as accommodating toward Turkey today as they were toward Iraq yesterday when it massacred the Kurds (and for the same commercial reasons), I await the mobilization of my parliamentary colleagues, of all defenders of freedom of expression, and of my feminist sisters.

5 August 1994

On Trial for Being a Kurd

On 8 December [1994], my trial (and that of my seven Kurdish parliamentary colleagues) will come to a close. That is the day the State Security Court of Ankara hands down its verdict. The public prosecutor of that Court, which was set up by the 1980 military dictatorship, has demanded the death penalty.

What crimes did we commit to deserve such punishment? Only one: bearing witness. Bearing witness to the great tragedy of the Kurdish people in Turkey. An indigenous people whose very existence has been negated and whose language, identity, and culture have been banned for seventy years. A people that has, as the victim of systematic cultural genocide, been subjected to a deliberate policy of depopulation of the countryside and destruction of its villages, forests, and traditional way of life, for the past several years. Even the Turkish Minister of Human Rights has admitted that in the past two years the Turkish army has evacuated and set fire to at least 1,390 Kurdish villages; and to date, at least two million Kurdish civilians have been displaced and abandoned to their fate. To this may be added the forced evacuation of some ten Kurdish towns and the exodus of five to six million Kurds to Western Turkey, because of state terrorism and the paralysis of the local economy by the war.

Could we, elected in 1991 by the Kurdish people to represent and defend their interests and aspirations, remain silent before this tragedy? Obviously not. Our responsibilities as members of Parliament and as citizens were to speak out, to bear witness, to explore every means of putting an end to this fearsome war that

This article appeared in the *Washington Post* on 5 December 1994; it has been slightly modified here. The *International Herald Tribune* republished it on 7 December 1994 under the title "A Test for Turkey: Liberty or Oppression for Kurds in Parliament?" The German daily *Suddeutsche Zeitung* republished it on 9 December 1994 under the title "Nur usere Meinung gesagt."

is tearing our country apart, to find a peaceful solution to the legitimate demands of the fifteen million Kurds in Turkey, within a framework of democracy and within existing borders.

Speaking freely in a country governed under an antidemocratic Constitution and laws that were imposed by a military dictatorship involves great risk, even for members of Parliament, whose job it is. Eighty-two leaders and members of our party, including my parliamentary colleague Mehmet Sincar, and 34 journalists and newspaper distributors have been murdered by death squads for having dared to bear witness and challenge the official, military version of events. For the same reason, 106 journalists, academics, and writers are in now prison. My husband, Mehdi Zana, former mayor of the main Kurdish city of Diyarbakir, who previously spent fifteen years in Turkish prisons for his beliefs, is now serving a four-year term for testifying before the European Parliament.

After barely escaping two attempts on my life, I have been held behind bars since 5 March [1994]. I am charged with (among other "crimes") appearing before panels of the U.S. Congressional Helsinki Commission and of the Carnegie Endowment for International Peace, with making statements on European television, and with speaking a Kurdish sentence in the Turkish Parliament about brotherhood between the Kurdish and Turkish peoples. Even the color of my clothes constituted a "crime of separatism" according to my Turkish inquisitors. My fellow members of Parliament are charged, imprisoned, and threatened with death for similar "crimes."

For the general public, our Kafkaesque trial has been a gripping example of how the Turkish political-legal system functions. After five months in custody on order of the public prosecutor, we finally appeared before the State Security Court in Ankara. The court then terminated the proceedings after only six purely formal hearings, during which all requests to call defense witnesses and experts and to confront prosecution witnesses were turned down. Observers sent by international nongovernmental organizations (NGOs), the European Parliament, and the Council of Europe unanimously agreed that we were being persecuted for voicing our opinions. They claimed that this was unacceptable in a state governed by law and calling itself democratic, and that we should be freed and our full rights restored. In the view of Ankara, the NGOs are suspect, indeed, they are probably secret terrorists, and even the Western governments are thought to have been brainwashed by the Kurds.

The Turkish authorities, prisoners of an obsolete kind of exclusive nationalism and afflicted with true paranoia about "Kurdish separatism," seem to want to use us, the elected representatives of the Kurdish people, as convenient scapegoats for the most serious economic, political, social, and moral crisis of Turkey's history. Things are going from bad to worse in this country corrupted by the exorbitant price of an absurd war that has already taken 15,000 lives and has cost the country at least seven million dollars. The military leaders and their puppet [Prime Minister] Mrs. Tansu Çiller would therefore like to offer their people a few token Kurdish victims.

At thirty-three, I have already undergone fourteen years of persecution, a dreadful experience of torture, and the unspeakable pain of the murder of a number of my close friends, including the old poet Musa Anter. These people wanted no more than to live in peace and democracy with the Turks, if the Turks would agree to respect Kurdish identity and culture. I have two children, a husband, and many dear friends. I love life and want to hold on to it. But my passion for justice for my tormented people, for their dignity and freedom, must be greater still. For of what value is a life of slavery, of humiliation and contempt for that which you hold most dear: your identity! I will therefore not give in to the Turkish Inquisition.

Beyond my own fate, I worry about the future of the Kurdish and Turkish peoples. Sending eight Kurdish members of Parliament to the gallows will not solve the acute problem of fifteen million Kurds—to which Turkey has mortgaged its future. By its extremism, the Turkish government risks involving the country in a general catastrophe for Kurds and for Turks. And for the West as well, which counts on Turkey as an outpost in a strategically important region.

The West must realize that Turkey is not only a territory for military bases and electronic eavesdropping. It is also a people torn by conflict and passion that could, like the Shah's Iran, slip into the irrational. If the hope of a peaceful solution to the Kurdish problem, embodied by us, members of Parliament of the Democracy Party [DEP], is killed by Turkey's warlords, then there is a great risk that the Kurds will turn en masse to the camp of violence and Islamic fundamentalism. And if the Kurds, geographically situated next to fundamentalist Iran, go in that direction, then all of Turkey will follow suit. This would be a misfortune for us all!

That is why, by persevering in our struggle for a peaceful settlement of the Kurdish problem in Turkey—within the framework of democracy and of the respect, not only for the existing borders but also for the dignity, identity, and equality of the two peoples who make up this country—we know we are serving the cause of regional peace and stability and are defending the universal values of civilization against the barbarity of religious and nationalist fundamentalism. We call on the people of the democratic countries to bear witness along with us. Tomorrow, if the irreparable is carried out, your governments—which remained silent about the martyrdom of the Iraqi Kurds until the very last moment—must not be able to claim ignorance of the Kurdish tragedy in Turkey.

5 December 1994

Before the Turkish Inquisition

Today, millions of Kurds, Turks and defenders of human rights and democracy and activists in women's movements around the world are turning their attention toward this courtroom. They are concerned about the fate of the Kurdish members of Parliament and the fate of the first Kurdish woman to be elected to Parliament; they have all been called before the Turkish Inquisition for having expressed the Kurdish people's aspirations to democracy and freedom, their sufferings and their tragedy. The observers, who come from around the world, lend a historic quality to this hearing.

As I have said before, I have no intention of defending myself. For I am a member of Parliament, freely elected by the will of the people. My supporters voted for me so that I would express and try to realize their wishes, their hopes and their demands. They alone can say whether I carried out my mission well. The only legitimate, democratic judgment that an elected representative of the people can accept is that of elections, the verdict of the ballot box. Aside from that—no court can judge me, and certainly not one set up by a Constitution and laws resulting from a military coup d'état that denied the universal principles of the rule of law and of democracy.

Many institutions that symbolize the public, democratic conscience of the civilized world—such as the European Parliament, the Council of Europe, Amnesty International, the International Federation for Human Rights, Helsinki Watch, and the Interna-

---

Translation of this article is courtesy of the Kurdish Institute of Paris. This declaration was to have been read on 8 December 1994 during the final hearing of the Ankara trial. However, in view of the way the trial had been conducted, with the Court making a mockery of the right to a fair trial, Leyla Zana's lawyers decided to boycott the hearing. Therefore, Leyla Zana decided not to read this text in Court.

tional Human Rights Law Group—are unanimous in thinking that the establishment and workings of this Court are incompatible with the principles of the rule of law and of democratic life. By thinking that you could condemn us after six summary hearings, on the basis of assertions and accusations that are merely figments of your imagination, without any respect for the most elementary rules of legal procedure and without the rights of the defense, you have shown the world the tragicomic system of justice in Turkish-style democracy and your impoverished ideology and ideas of law and justice, incompatible with those of the civilized world.

As a result, some people consider the State Security Courts to be special institutions, at the orders of the military General Staff, that are charged with the execution of prisoners of conscience. To me, they are courts of the Inquisition of the Atatürk sect. This sect, which denies the existence of the Kurdish people and its culture and adopts a fanatical cult of Turkish nationalism, has imposed its principles by force on the Constitution and laws. The State Security Courts are courts of opinion that consider all those who dare think freely, untrammeled by those (Kemalist) principles—who propose political and cultural pluralism, who defend the civilized idea of a state without official ideology, impartial, democratic and at the service of the people—as dangerous enemies. They claim the right to punish them, they create an intellectual reign of terror and throw into jail the free minds, the intellectuals, journalists, and writers of our country.

Turkish heir of the infamous Torquemada of the Spanish Inquisition, your Chief Inquisitor, Nusret Demiral, who sees "separatist traitors" and "terrorists" in all those who dare mention the word *Kurd* or who evoke the existence, identity, and legitimate democratic rights of the Kurdish people, has demanded the death sentence for us. I do not want to argue with that "gentleman," nor with a jury taking orders from the hidden and shady forces that, although not elected, direct the state and claim the right to judge us, the elected members of Parliament who represent the will of the people. I would like briefly to set out my views of this Turkish-style democracy, reduced to vassalage, in the shadow the bayonet, that is responsible for the tragic impasse in that my country finds itself today.

At no moment in its history has Turkey been able to experience a pluralist democracy. To this day all its Constitutions have been imposed by the Armed Forces. For twenty-seven years this country lived under the regime of a single party and a National Leader—a sort of Turkish fascism. In the 1982 Constitution, imposed by the military regime, Kemal Atatürk is described as "immortal chief, unparalleled hero." This Constitution adopts "the reforms, and principles of Atatürk" as the official ideology of the state. The Constitution stipulaties that "no opinion, no consideration can be protected against the nationalism, the principles and reforms, and the civilizing acts of Atatürk"—freedom of opinion and expression is limited in a fascistic manner.

The state clearly has an official, totalitarian ideology, and that ideology is "Atatürkism." Turkey today is the only member of the Council of Europe to have an official state ideology. The founder of this ideology is the subject of a cult; busts and statues of him are erected in even the most isolated corners of the country; and his name is given to schools, avenues, hospitals, dams, and airports. In democracy there is no place for saviors, for eternal national leaders, or for the cult of the personality. For this reason the French Constitution did not adopt Gaullism as an official ideology and the United States did not make a cult figure of its revolutionary war hero, George Washington. One only sees such actions in countries that clearly reject pluralist democracy, such as Stalin's Russia, Mussolini's Italy, and Franco's Spain.

The Turkish Politburo is the National Security Council, composed of senior military commanders and a few civilian leaders who remain timidly in the background of the military brass. To this day, the "recommendations" of this Council have, without exception, been diligently adopted, unaltered by the Government and the Parliament. In democratic societies the overwhelming majority of the people do not even know the name of the Army Chief of Staff, who is merely an official of the Ministry of Defense; but in Turkish-style democracy the true head of state, the Pope or Sheikh-ul-Islam of the Atatürk Sect, the General Secretary of the State Party is the Chief of Staff of the Armed Forces.

Even the late President Turgut Özal himself, before proposing his projects on civil political life for public debate, used to say "I've discussed it with the army; they are not opposed," thus showing that they felt obliged to exercise their right of *fetwa* (approval). [Prime Minister] Mrs. Tansu Çiller boasted of having prepared her "democratization package" with General Güres, the Chief of Staff. In reminding you of this, my aim is to show that Turkish democracy has only a limited and supervised parliamentary rule, incompatible with universal standards of democracy. The judgment handed down to us had already been decided by the Chief of Staff General Güres in press statements. The Prime Minister was then charged with the task of getting these directives rapidly through Parliament, and this Court of Inquisition has the task of supplying a fig leaf to cover the legal scandal.

This artificial parliamentarianism that they try to carry out within the framework of a Constitution born of a military coup d'état, and of Atatürk nationalism based on a denial of the Kurdish people, is designed merely to fool public opinion. The present Turkish political parties have, basically, no major differences. So it is not surprising that Mrs. Çiller, though governing in a coalition with the Social Democratic Populist Party [SHP],[1] cooperates with Türkes,[2] flirts with Ecevit,[3] and bargains with Yilmaz.[4] Beyond the conflicts of interest and ambition among individuals and groups, all of these parties are parties of the established order, authorized by the General Staff and sharing the same basic nationalist ideology. The People's Labor Party [HEP] and the Democracy Party [DEP] which have striven to develop an alternative pluralist democracy outside this framework, and which through dialogue and debate seek a solution that is vital to Turkey, were immediately banned. I would not be surprised if the Welfare Party [Refah, or RP], which tries to act outside the limits of this barrack-room democracy, were also banned by the Constitutional Court.[5]

It is common knowledge that the present chairman of this Court is someone who openly supported and congratulated the Junta, that took power by coup d'état in 1980, dissolved Parliament and the political parties, overthrew the legitimate government, threw out the Constitution then in force, jailed and tortured tens of thousands of people and imposed a horrifying reign of terror on the country. The other members of this Court kept silent and carried on their affairs throughout that painful ordeal. The chairman of the Parliament, Mr. Cindoruk, was quite right in questioning the respectability and legitimacy of this institution. Similarly, Mr. Cindoruk's belated discovery that the Turkish Parliament is not a democratic Parliament is highly pertinent.

When the paths of legal struggle are blocked, people tend to resort to other methods—violence and war. The Algerian tragedy and the tragedy the Kurds in our country are living once again confirm this universal truth. Pluralism and democracy are vital for Turkey because of its culture, its sociological realities, its heritage, and its traditions. But some forces, which consider the country as their private property, want to lock Turkey into a rigid, narrow, sterile mould of fanatical nationalism. They want to make Atatürk their private domain and transform Turkey into *Atatürkey*; by their use of repressive methods of another age, these people have brought the country to the deepest social, political, and moral crisis of its history.

Turkey should consider the Kurds a people with their own language, identity, and culture; they are entitled, within a democratic framework and within existing borders, to enjoy political and cultural rights and the same property rights as the Turks, thereby ensuring the internal peace, stability, and development of the country. But Turkish nationalists trample underfoot universal human values and the obligations they have assumed under international treaties and pursue a fantasy of forcible dispersion of the Kurdish people and destruction of its national and cultural character by turning the Kurds into Turks. All the resources of the country are devoted to military expenditure, to a policy that consists of making brothers kill brothers in pursuit of this horrible dream. In the Middle Ages the Catholic kings of Spain, in order to forcibly purify their country of all religious and ethnic minorities, instituted the Inquisitorial Courts and ordered the minorities to chose between "baptism or exodus." For the last seventy years in Atatürkey, Kurds have been forced to chose between becoming Turkish and exile. Kurds wishing to preserve their honor and identity must choose guerrilla warfare, jail, the scaffold, or emigration to the West. The Kurdish people have spent forty-eight of the Republic's seventy-one-year history under extralegal and repressive regimes, under states of siege or emergency laws. Those who want to defend their identity are considered enemies of the state and are annihilated in one way or another.

This fanatical state is hostile to our language; but every bird prefers to sing in its own way. How can speaking and writing in our own language, one of the oldest Indo-European languages in the world, transmitting it to our children, singing our songs in our own language, and learning and teaching Kurdish be harmful to the Turkish people? When they use their language in all walks of life, do we make any comments?

As the democratic representative of a people who believe in political and cultural pluralism, who subscribe to the Universal Declaration of Human Rights, I said, in my first speech at the Parliament, that I did not approve of the antidemocratic 1982 Constitution imposed on the country by a coup d'état, and I said a few words in Kurdish in favor of the brotherhood of the Kurdish and Turkish peoples. Even these few words, because they were spoken in Kurdish, were considered too much. Are we not equally children of this country? Moreover, we are an indigenous people who have lived on these lands since the earliest recorded time. Is it a crime to speak of humanity and brotherhood in our own language and our own country? Is it not rather these prohibitions and restrictions, the practice of cultural genocide against the Kurdish people, that constitutes a crime against humanity? For seventy years the hard-pressed Kurdish people, the majority of whom do not understand Turkish, have been able to bear the fact that you always address them in Turkish—do you find it so unbearable that the first Kurdish woman elected to Parliament should address you for just two minutes in Kurdish? Is that your idea of tolerance, of humanity, of democracy, and of civilization, Oh Turkish leaders? If you ban the language, culture, and identity of millions of people, if by means of brute force and laws that institutionalize state violence, you prevent them from expressing their grievances and aspirations by legal means, these people will, sooner or later, revolt to try and defend their dignity and identity.

Since 1924 Turkey has lived under the rule of these inhuman prohibitions, and it is constantly struggling against tension and convulsion. Turkey, which is fiftieth in the world in terms of per capita income, maintains the sixth or seventh largest army in the world. Our army exceeds the British, German, French, and Japanese armies in personnel. Why do we need such a huge army? No doubt to repress possible uprisings by the Kurdish people, deprived of freedom, whom you are trying forcibly to silence. For this reason the lion's share of our country's resources is devoted to military expenditures. According to official figures, in 1993 Turkey was the largest importer of arms in the world. In 1994 nearly half of its budget, that is, 401 trillion liras out of 890 trillion, were allocated to military expenditures. The arms bought with these astronomical sums, earned by the labor of our people, are used to kill our own people, our own children.

Our prime minister, Mrs. Tansu Çiller, rejoices at the death of young Kurds. She thinks that if a few more thousand people are killed the Kurdish problem will be settled once and for all. This woman studied in the United States for several years. But she has, apparently, only learned business or rather the art of rapid personal enrichment by speculation and corruption. It is a pity that she did not think of learning the democratic and human values of freedom and pluralism from American society. I learned from my mother, who was illiterate but imbued with Kurdish traditional culture, that the people of the "seventy-two nations," whatever their beliefs, their race, or the color of their skins, were equal because they were all created by God, and that one should respect their language, identity, and traditions. Our tradition is that of the deep humanism of the Kurdish Sultan Saladin, who has come down through history as a symbol of tolerance and humanism. It is not the tradition of Attila, Gengis Khan, or Selim the Cruel, who had 40,000 innocents put to the sword in order to terrorize the local people, or of the Ottoman sultans, who murdered their own children and brothers to consolidate power, or of Mustafa Kemal, who sent to the gallows all the Kurdish lords who, in his time of need, had generously come to his help. In your history books you present these people as symbols of Turkish nationalism and boast of them. For this reason, for me, for us, the young Kurds in the mountains are, equally with the Turkish soldiers, sent to fight them, all our children. The death of every one of them causes me pain and in our collective spirit, opens up wounds that are hard to heal.

The war is, from the point of view of the Kurdish people, a great tragedy. Thousands of dead, tens of thousands of prisoners and victims of torture, millions of Kurds uprooted from their land, their homes, without work, without anything, abandoned to hunger and misery. Mountain villages and forests set on fire, towns evacuated, and a militia system that forces brother to kill brother. This tragedy should shame people who have any feeling for their share of humanity and should cause them to reflect.

We are born of this people; we share the same destiny. As members of Parliament we have tried with all our might to stop the war, to silence the guns, and to create a climate in which people can discuss their problems and seek to resolve them by dialogue in a democratic context.

As a result of these efforts, in the last period of Mr. Özal's presidency, positive steps were taken in the direction of social compromise and peace. But war lords and pashas, who profit from the continuation of war and violence (those forces determined to maintain and justify their power and economic interests by war), got the upper hand over the supporters of peace, at any rate for the moment. These forces, like the clever thief putting the owner of the robbed house in the wrong, want to silence and try us, members of Parliament who support peace and democracy, to put us behind bars for having attempted to make known the sufferings and tragedy of our people to public opinion in Turkey and in the rest of the world. A Parliament in which more than 150 members are wanted for common-law offenses, such as stealing, swindling, smuggling, and corruption, has been able, under the leadership of a prime minister whose name has been linked with all sorts of financial scandals, to lift our parliamentary immunity, and has, in doing so, lost all respect and all legitimacy in the eyes of public opinion. The Constitutional Court, made up of judges who, in the main, supported the junta, also supported this decision and then, with a logic unprecedented in the world, banned our party on the grounds of views our president is said to have expressed abroad and of a Peace Appeal our party had made—this same Court declared that we were henceforth also stripped of our membership in Parliament. It is certain that those judgments contradict modern conceptions of Law, of the European Convention on Human Rights, and of the final Act of the Helsinki and Paris Charters, all of which Turkey has signed. For this reason, our lawyers are suing Turkey before the European Commission on Human Rights. The Commission has accepted their plea and decided on emergency measures to start its inquiries. We expect that the Commission will announce its findings in the next few weeks, and its judgment,[6] against which there is no appeal, will be very embarrassing for Turkey. The terms of international treaties take precedence over those of the Constitution and Turkish laws, and they are very restrictive.

Thus, we are convinced that once public opinion and international organizations recognize that we are in the right, all the judgments against us announced to date will be overturned by the European Court of Human Rights. Law and justice will prevail. It is impossible that this independent European Court, without any ideological prejudices, charged with pronouncing on the Law and applying universal rules of law, could permit citizens to be tried for having used the words "Kurdish people" or "Kurdistan," without resorting to violence, and for having claimed the legitimate rights of the Kurdish people. The "crime of opinion" is a disgrace that the civilized world will not be able to accept.

Your Inquisitorial Court, whose purposes are not to establish law and truth but to judge, through us, a whole people and to intimidate the Kurdish people, has rejected all requests to call witnesses or expert evidence, or inquiries by our lawyers. At Strasbourg, through the intermediary evidence of historians, documents, and experts, the following witnesses will be quoted: the Seljuk Sultan Togrul Bey, who, in 1150, long before us, used the word "Kurdistan"; the Sultan Selim the Cruel, who signed a treaty of alliance with the Kurdish governments of his time; Süleyman the Magnificent, who, in a letter to King François I of France boasted that he was sovereign of Kurdistan; the Sultan Abdul Hamid, who had a Kurdistan medal struck; and Mustafa Kemal. When in difficulty, Mustafa Kemal called for help from and kissed the hands of Kurdish religious leaders and proposed the creation of a "Province of Kurdistan" to the Parliament in 1922. After his victory, which was achieved thanks to the major contribution made by the Kurdish people, he sent to the gallows the Kurdish leaders who had come to his aid. This trial against us will become a trial of the nationalist ideology and of the Turkish government before world public opinion. Those who think they can silence us in our own country by violence and brute force will not be able to prevent law and justice being demonstrated before world public opinion.

Our struggle based on law will be the natural extension, on an international level, of the struggle for peace and democracy that we are trying to conduct in difficult conditions. It is not, if you will excuse the term, to save our heads that we are doing this, but to win recognition in the international Courts of law of the rights of the Kurdish people, victims of one of the greatest injustices of the twentieth century, and for the legitimacy of our struggle.

Unless it wishes to be isolated from the international community, as are Iraq, Iran, Libya, and Serbia, Turkey must respect the treaties it has signed. These treaties guarantee freedom of opinion and the rights of minorities. For this reason, the verdicts of Inquisitorial Courts set up under the laws of the military junta are incompatible with European law, are completely invalid, and will cost the state dearly.

I would like to add only one thing to this. I am thirty-three years old; I have already passed fourteen years of my life in front of the gates of prisons, subject to various threats and pressures. I was arrested once and suffered barbaric torture. My husband has spent fifteen years of his life in prison for his opinions. We have not surrendered, and we will not surrender. I am a woman who has gone beyond fear and the fear of death—I live beyond that.

I am inspired in my struggle by other passions. I am not afraid of your generals, nor of your Courts, nor of your laws of a bygone age, nor of your gallows. In spite of my suffering and trials, I love life. The people I love are numerous, and perhaps those who love me are as well. But my passion for justice, my determination to contribute to the struggle to allow my people to lead an existence that is worthwhile, free, and dignified, and that respects its identity, comes first. You cannot suppress ideas and aspirations adopted by millions of people by putting a few people or even a few thousand to death. Were those who crucified Jesus, burned Joan of Arc at the stake, and condemned Galileo able to prevent the spread of their ideas? Only fourteen years ago Leyla Zana was an ordinary young peasant girl whose world was limited to the search for a little domestic happiness. The events that followed the coup d'état and the barbarities she suffered have made her an activist with a will of steel. Were you to burn her or hang her, there would be millions of Kurdish women, tens of thousands of Leyla Zanas, who would rise up before you to carry on the struggle.

My real preoccupation today is the future of this country, of the Kurdish and Turkish peoples. The sentencing of the Kurdish members of Parliament will mean that henceforth the path of democratic struggle is closed to the Kurdish people and that the partisans of war and violence will be reinforced, the country will be drawn into a civil war that will be a major disaster for the two peoples. Let those who think that setting fire to Kurdistan will resolve the problem not be too surprised if, tomorrow, confrontation and explosion break out in Istanbul, Izmir, Adana, or Mersin. Let them ponder well the words of Shimon Peres, the Israeli Minister of Foreign Affairs, during his visit to Turkey. "After years of war, although we are assured of absolute superiority in all domains, we have reached the conclusion that peace with the Palestinians is a necessity, because it is not possible to live with the hatred of two million people." In the same way, Turkey, even if it depopulates Kurdistan, even if it creates the most powerful army in the world, will not be able to live long with the hatred of fifteen million Kurds—it will not be able to attain peace and stability. The only solution is to turn over this sad page and accept the fact that Turkey is the common country of two different peoples, Kurdish and Turkish, each with a specific language, culture, and identity, and to seek, through democratic dialogue, to put into practice a settlement that will let these peoples live in peace, democracy, and equality, with respect for the rights and identity of each other. Understand this well—there will be no victor in a civil war between Kurds and Turks.

It will only end in catastrophe for both peoples; whereas with a compromise freely arrived at, by consent, persuasion, and dialogue, both peoples will win. For this we must conquer mutual prejudice, fear, and the narrow nationalism of a bygone age, the collective paranoid separatism ingrained in society. It will take a long time to convince our Turkish neighbors, with their weak democratic tradition and militaristic tradition, who even recently had no word in their language for compromise. It will not be easy to repair the damage caused by seventy years of brainwashing and ideological conditioning. Like Nelson Mandela, who set himself to educating those who had thrown him into jail, we Kurds, despite all of our sufferings, will have to educate our Turkish neighbors, tell them we love them and wish to live with them, but as equals. We must get them to understand that a people's defense of its existence and identity does not constitute an act of hostility or betrayal.

I would like to end this statement by recalling an incident that occurred in 1989 during a first conference of dialogue between South Africans organized in Paris by Mme. Danielle Mitterrand.[7] In the course of this week-long meeting, a Black leader, in spite of the difficulty, established a dialogue with the White judge who had sentenced him to fifteen years in jail. They found that their views on the future of the country were not all that different. The judge said to the Black leader: "I condemned you for aiming to set up a Communist dictatorship based on Black domination. We were worried that once in power you would either drive out or massacre the Whites. But, in fact, you just wanted to live with us in the same country in a pluralist democracy. If I had known then that you were sincere in your convictions, I would not have condemned you. Our people would not have experienced so much suffering, spilled so much blood and tears. I really do apologize."

One day, will the many civil and military judges come and apologize to us for the suffering they have inflicted on us, our families, and our people? I am convinced that if not us, then our children will enjoy that free future.

Our struggle aims at preparing for such a future, at beginning a new period in Kurdish-Turkish relations, a new tradition based on mutual respect. I am convinced that we will win this struggle for civilization, peace, and democracy and against barbarity and the advocates of war and hate.

With this certainty I respectfully greet you.

8 December 1994

1. Social Democrat Populist Party, left-wing Kemalist.
2. Alpaslan Türkes is a retired Colonel of the Turkish Army. After World War II he was convicted of spreading Nazi ideas and collaborating with Hitler's Germany, but then was reintegrated into the army. He helped engineer the 1960 military coup d'état and founder of the neo-fascist Nationalist Action Party [MHP] and of its militia, the Grey Wolves (Bozkurt), which has been implicated in the murder of students and civilians in Turkey and in the attack on Pope John Paul II.
3. Bulent Ecevit is former president of the Republican People's Party [CHP], former prime minister of Turkey, and current vice prime minister and president of the Democratic Left Party [DSP]. His position is one of extreme Turkish nationalism and the ideology of the Turkish state; he fiercely rejects all recognition of the existence of the Kurds in Turkey.
4. Mesut Yilmaz is president of the conservative Motherland Party [ANAP], which was in the opposition in 1994. He is currently (1998) prime minister.
5. This prediction proved to be correct; the Welfare Party (Refah, or RP) was indeed banned on 16 January 1998.
6. On 26 November 1997 the European Court for Human Rights ruled against Turkey in the first part of the appeal made by Leyla Zana and five other Kurdish former members of Parliament. Their appeal dealt with the issue of their arrest and detention in March 1994. The Court unanimously judged that Turkey had violated three Articles (5.3, 5.4, and 5.5) of the European Convention on Human Rights relating to right to trial within a reasonable delay, right of appeal of the legality of arrest or detention, and right to compensation in conditions of arrest or detention contrary to the provisions of the articles. The Court ordered Turkey to pay damages to and reimburse the legal expenses of Mrs. Zana and the others. The Court judged that Article 15 of the Convention, providing for suspension of some freedoms in emergency situations that endanger the nation's life and security, invoked by the Turkish party in its defense, was not applicable in this case, in which elected representatives of the people were arrested in Ankara, the country's capital. The Court's ruling on this first part of the case of the Kurdish MPs is already, in itself, a stinging condemnation of the Turkish authorities. It comes three and a half years after the appeal made by the MPs' defense lawyers, who are now waiting for the verdict on the main issue of the case, namely, the heavy prison sentences passed on elected representatives for "crimes" of opinion. (Adapted from International Committee for the Liberation of the Kurdish Parliamentarians Imprisoned in Turkey (CILDEKT) Bulletin #79, 27 November 1997)
7. President and founder of Fondation France-Libertés.

Letter to Danielle Mitterrand
President and Founder, Fondation France-Libertés

31 March 1994

Dear Danielle:

I received your precious letter and the pen you sent me and am very happy to have them. Yours was the first letter I received in prison.

As you may remember, when we saw each other in Paris I told you what might happen in the near future. We were therefore not very surprised by what did happen to us.

I know the Turkish government well, a knowledge which I did not get from books, but from everyday experience. Since 1980, the government has put me through many ordeals. But even so, I never imagined that it would go so far in trampling its own laws. On the one hand, it proclaims to the world that "the justice system is independent of us," while on the other, it acknowledges its own interference in the judicial system. [Prime minister] Mrs. Tansu Çiller's election campaign was based entirely on the issue of lifting our parliamentary immunity, and in every campaign meeting she boasted of having "thrown the DEP [Democracy Party] parliamentarians out of Parliament."

I have been meaning to write you since I returned from Paris, as I wanted to thank you for your interest and support. But we didn't even have a chance to catch our breath. On 2 March , there was a sort of coup d'état. We were surrounded by the police even before the vote on lifting our parliamentary immunity had taken place. Three police cars tailed me as I was going to the airport to welcome Ségolène Royal, the member of Parliament whom you had sent, and I was forced to turn back.

When we reached Parliament I heard that Mr. [Hatip] Dicle, the president of our party, had been arrested. Barely two minutes later, our colleague Orhan Dogan was arrested before our very eyes. The police grabbed him by the nape of the neck and pushed him into a car. We then understood the extreme gravity of the situation and locked ourselves into the Parliament building. The Parliament was besieged.

We remained shut up there until 4 March when we were brought to the State Security Court. The Court sent us to the police's antiterrorist section. We were kept there until 16 March when, at 6:00 A.M., we were taken to Court. After making us wait until 6:00 P.M for nothing, without questioning us, they took us to the head office of Security, where we spent the night of 16 March. On 17 March, we were sent back to the Court, which decided to lock us up.

While we were detained, we did not suffer any physical abuse, but they tried to destroy us psychologically. I am convinced that without your unremitting efforts and the intervention of M. [François] Mitterrand, we would have been tortured. It was your action that blocked them from having recourse to torture.

On 17 March, we were brought to prison. The first night, which I spent locked up in a filthy sort of dungeon, was unbearable. The next day I went to see the prison director and told him that I could not stay in a place like that. I was transferred to a room that already held some forty common-law criminals. It was impossible to find a corner where I might read or write. I spent a week there. Thanks to the fact that my parliamentary colleagues spoke to certain ministers, I was transferred to an individual cell. I am very relieved to be in the new place, where at least I can read and write.

I will be staying here for the rest of my term in prison, unless our party is outlawed and we lose the status of parliamentarians. However, as long as I remain in this cell, I will write you often.

My dear mother, I am truly touched that you accept me as your daughter. I feel very lucky to have a combative mother who fights for oppressed peoples struggling for their freedom. I wholeheartedly believe in a better future for oppressed, excluded peoples, and in the end of oppressive regimes.

In my life, I have never chosen the easy way out. The easy way out is, after all, within everyone's reach. What counts is overcoming difficulty. In my country, the struggle for peace, brotherhood, and democracy comes with a high price. But we are prepared. If only there were peace, so that we could finally have true brotherhood! And stop the bloodshed! If only the people finally had some happiness, and mothers no longer had to mourn their dead, and children no longer had to suffer humiliation!

I know that you are doing great things for us. That is why I do not want to take up too much of your time. I will try to be worthy both of my own oppressed people, and of you—a fighter for freedom.

My sincere thanks, and my regards to you and to the President. In the hope of seeing you again soon.

Letter to Danielle Mitterrand

President and Founder, Fondation France-Libertés

21 April 1994

My dear Mother:

I am so happy to call you Mother. I have just received your third letter. Full of the joy of reading it, I am hurrying to answer you right away. By sharing my days in prison, you are giving me strength. Your concern and your action fill me with hope.

Whenever I see my parliamentary colleagues we talk about you and what you are doing. Kendal [Nezan, President of Kurdish Institute in Paris] keeps us posted about your important activities. We were even able to get a Turkish translation of your statement to the press [in New York] and of your Peace Appeal. Our only worry is not to wear you out with our problems.

I think that at no other time in history has the Kurdish question emerged so clearly onto the world scene. We need to realize the importance of this, and indeed we are very much aware of it.

We do not want to take advantage of anyone's good will. We will defend the coexistence of our two peoples on the basis of equality, and we will defend democracy, human rights, and freedom for the country future's. There is a good likelihood that in the near future our Democracy Party [DEP] will be outlawed. Motivated by our faith in democracy, we are preparing to create a new party. The Turkish democrats and the oppressed Kurdish people need one. We will try to fulfill this need as best we can.

Turkey finds itself in a major impasse on the social, political, and economic levels. This impasse is the result of seven decades of bad political decisions. The country is in the grip of a grave social crisis caused by an economy adrift. The rate of criminality is increasing every day. In the last two weeks, ten women charged with murder have arrived in our prison. They were arrested for killing their children or husbands, for economic reasons. They are the victims of other people's political mistakes. I talk to about ten women every day, particularly to the women who work in the prison. They are, for the most part, married and have children. They burst into tears, saying: "We can no longer make ends meet the way things are now. We can't give our families what they need. We are being crushed by our burdens." Hearing their stories fills me with sorrow. It is always the ones at the bottom of the ladder who pay for the errors of those on top. I don't think the people will be able to take these policies much longer. Members of Parliament from various parties who come to see us in prison all think that "political mistakes have brought Turkey to the current impasse."

My dear mother, another subject that frightens me is the intervention of Turkish forces in southern Kurdistan. On the pretext of "mopping up the PKK [kurdistan Workers' Party]", they treat the local population ruthlessly and set people against each other. Moreover, Turkey is now making efforts to reestablish relations with Saddam Hussein. Turkey has never wanted to recognize the federated state of southern Kurdistan, and it is obvious that it is going to engage in all sorts of intrigues.

The recent position taken by Europe—the demand for democratic reforms—upsets Turkey but also makes it reflect. While telling Europe "not to interfere in our internal affairs," Turkey requests intervention in Bosnia and Karabagh. But no one ever asks the Turks, "Why are you interfering in the internal affairs of others?" The Turks have many contradictions. They have signed a number of international treaties and conventions but do not really apply any of them; and they have the nerve to claim to be defenders of democracy and human rights. With them, everything is window dressing, even democracy. Last month, they seemed to be trying to stop the migration of Kurds from Kurdistan toward the western part of the country. They realize that when the Kurds immigrate to the Turkish cities they bring their problems with them, especially their identity problem, and that fact is highly disturbing to the Turkish government. At first, the government encouraged people to leave; now, they stop them from emigrating. Last week, Kurds who emigrated to Istanbul, Izmir, Adana, and Mersin came to see us. They said: "Don't worry; even if no Kurds remain in Kurdistan, we will carry on our struggle here." I was particularly moved by the enthusiasm of the women, who said: "Don't worry! We're with you to the end." This really made me think.

The day that I can serve others, as you do, I will be happy. But for that day to come, I must work hard, read a lot, and live long, since there is such a great distance to travel.

I would like to tell you a little about my daily life. I think that you want me to also. I wake up every morning at seven o'clock to the sound of the iron door. That is when my guard changes. Two women leave, and two others replace them. At eight o'clock, roll call begins. After counting all the other prisoners one by one, they knock at the door of my cell, where I am all alone. I think that they put me in an individual cell for security reasons. When the cell door opens, my heart races; the opening door sounds like a bomb. For a second I think I must be in Kurdistan. When I realize that it is only the door, I can breathe again. Then I am given the daily papers. After I read them, I have breakfast. I clean up my cell and at around eleven o'clock I am allowed to walk for an hour in the courtyard. Back in my cell, I begin reading. I have all kinds of reading material—magazines, novels, and other books.

Around two o'clock in the afternoon I am brought to the prison's administration building to see my lawyers. My colleagues, the other imprisoned members of Parliament, are also there. We stay in the visitors' room for about three hours. Then we all go back to our cells. I prepare my dinner, which I share with the guards. After doing the dishes I watch the news on television. Then I sit at my table and answer letters and cards from friends. It is hard to sleep in prison. The lights are on all night, and it hurts your eyes. So I sometimes stay up all night. Without books it would be unbearable. That is how I spend my days now. Excuse me for going on so long about it.

You say you would like me to learn French. I asked my family to bring me books, tapes, and other necessary material. I will try hard to learn. You cannot imagine how much I want to learn your language as fast as possible, to be able to talk with you more easily.

Thanking you over and over for your interest in me, and for everything you have done for me, I send you my regards and affection, and hope to see you again very soon.

Your daughter who loves and admires you.

P.S. Many, many thanks for the red roses!

Letter to Ségolène Royal

Former French Minister of the Environment;
Current French Minister of Education for Primary and
Secondary School (since 1997)

26 April 1994

Dear Ségolène:

I am taking advantage of my son Ronay's visit to send you this letter, since he will be returning to France for his studies,

I would like to thank you again for your solidarity. Thanks to the fact that you were at our side at the crucial moment, we were spared the worst. We were neither molested nor tortured. Because of your testimony and your intervention, our situation became known to the public, which permitted the internationalization of a problem that the government would have preferred to resolve in its own way, that is, in secret, accusing us of all kinds of crimes.

The first thirteen days, which we spent in the antiterrorist section, were psychologically highly stressful. Then, on the very day that your Minister of Foreign Affairs came to Ankara, when some thought we would be freed and judged as free defendants as a good will gesture toward France—the homeland of human rights—the government decided to incarcerate us, to demonstrate that it does not confuse a legal case with human rights.

I spent the first night in prison in a kind of dank cave crawling with vermin, without doors or windows. I read later in the press that that night, your minister made a speech on Turkey's commitment to democracy and a just state. I could not understand how anyone could lower himself to that extent just to expand a market!

I then spent a week in a large room that I shared with forty-three other prisoners, all criminals, arrested for such crimes as murder, theft, and prostitution. Finally, thanks to the help of fellow members of Parliament, I was transferred to an individual cell, and I was finally able to get some peace. I am allowed to read newspapers, once a week I receive family visits, and our lawyers come and see us frequently. Otherwise, the only people

I talk to are my two guards. I spend most of my time reading and writing.

We still do not know the date of the trial because the accusations against us have not yet been prepared. In a just state, people are arrested only when the charges against them are serious. In Turkey, they begin by incarcerating those they find undesirable, and then they order the prosecutors to gather testimony or "evidence" against them, to justify sentencing them to prison.

Thus, several military prosecutors have been given the responsibility of finding evidence of our guilt. They went to Kurdistan to question prisoners under torture, people who have "repented," and police auxiliaries. We are awaiting the follow-up. Probably by the end of May [1994] we will know the date of the trial, which could take place during the summer vacation.

We all are in good spirits. We know we are defending democracy and a better future for our people. Current Turkish policy has brought the country to the brink of bankruptcy and civil war. Public opinion is increasingly supportive of us. We know that it is not easy to win one's rights and freedom. Everything has a price, and we are paying it.

The solidarity of friends like you cheers us. Beyond the barriers of language and borders, I feel that you are a sister of the heart, even if we saw each other only for a few hours. If you have time, write to me, tell me about yourself, your family, your struggles, your ideas. Give the letters to my friend Kendal Nezan, who will know how to get them to me. Your letters will give me great pleasure, and will enable me to join you in thought. I will find a way to answer your letters. Thank you again for everything.

With my warmest regards,

Letter to My Daughter, Ruken

14 May 1994

My dear daughter:

It was on a day very much like today, on 14 May 1981, that you came into the world. You arrived at a time when I had many problems, but you made my troubles disappear. I will never forget that when you opened your eyes, I began to cry, because I was all alone in a little room in a maternity ward in Ankara. I began to ask myself questions. Why am I alone at all the difficult moments of my life? Will I be able to deal with the problems? Here I am, twenty years old, with two children and almost no one to help me. But after a few moments I stopped crying, and began to reproach myself for my attitude. Even alone, I had to stand on my own two feet, head held high. I began to take courage. Naturally, it would not be easy to remain upright. I would have to struggle, and that demanded awareness, determination, and conviction. But all that would come with a price. In my life, I always paid dearly for everything. In my search for knowledge and freedom, I have confronted all kinds of assault—insult, physical attack, and hunger. What we suffer from is often the result of ignorance.

Dear heart, I do not say this to make you unhappy. But life is pitiless, and we must know how to fight, otherwise we'll end up defeated by life. I want you to do well in school, to read a lot. I don't want you to be ignorant. Every human being needs knowledge. You have your whole life ahead of you, and you can give your life meaning if you are able to live fully and are aware of what you do.

I believe, my daughter, that you are going abroad next week and you will be beginning a new life. Everything new is both attractive and difficult. You can overcome problems only by discussing them with someone. If you don't talk them over, they will become more and more serious, to the point at which you can no longer overcome them. And what is more, in your new environment, you have to make a good impression and not be trouble to anyone.

I would so much like to be with you today, on you birthday. But don't worry, we have a long life before us. We will have many birthdays to celebrate together. I wish you a happy birthday and send you many hugs and kisses, my heart.

Thousands of kisses!

Your mother, who loves you very much.

Letter to My Son, Ronay

30 June 1994

My dear:

I decided to write you this letter in Kurdish. I hope it won't be hard for you to read your mother tongue.[1]

My heart, believe me, right now you are my main concern. I am sorry that you are unhappy in France. But you know as well as I do that we really have no other choice. You know what our situation is here. The family will soon have to give up the apartment in the housing for members of Parliament. Even if you came here, where would you stay? I know you are in love with B. I was never opposed to that relationship; on the contrary, I am glad you are in love. Moreover, I have respect for all love.

But we must see our own reality clearly. If we ignore our own reality, then, whether we want to or not, we make serious mistakes. Though I am sure that at age eighteen you are entirely capable of telling right from wrong, I still want to give you some advice. If you want to help yourself, your girl friend, your friends and companions, you must continue in school and do well in your studies.

Dear heart, while I write this letter I have a photo of you and your sister in front of me. I look at the photo while I write, since it does me good to look at your pictures. Ruken has grown a lot, and last week she wrote a letter to your father and me. I know she must be sad so far from us, but to keep us from worrying, she says that she's very happy with her trip to the United States. Sometimes, for the sake of those you are with, you must try to appear happy.

Child of my heart, we are doing very well; don't be worried about us. A few days ago we received the prosecutors' act of accusation. It is inconsistent and there is nothing legal in it. It is simply politically motivated. For that reason, our conviction or acquittal will depend on political considerations. Don't worry about it at all; we are ready for anything. You must know the proverb that says: "He fell into the pit he dug for his friend." For the moment, those who wish to judge us have made themselves ridiculous in the eyes of the public.

Apple of my eye! Take care of yourself. You live only once. Don't worry about us; enjoy your life. Don't forget that I love you very much. I hug you very tight. Give my regards to everyone who asks about me.

Your mother, who loves you very much.

---

1. Since the teaching of Kurdish is forbidden in Turkey, the Kurds must learn to read and write Kurdish on their own, often clandestinely.

Message to the Jury of the Norwegian Raftos Prize for Human Rights

22 October 1994

Dear Friends:

I am writing you this brief note even though I do not know whether it will reach you in time, since my letters are often confiscated. In my country, freedom of communication, like other freedoms, is subject to the arbitrary decision of the authorities.

I am very moved by the Human Rights prize with which you have honored me. My feelings are a mixture of joy and sorrow. I am glad that the struggle that I, in my own modest way, carry out against torture, for the respect of human dignity, for the recognition of the identity of my people, and for coexistence between Kurds and Turks, in democracy and with respect for the rights of each, should be acknowledged thousand of miles from my home, in a country like Norway. I am very grateful to you. But I feel sorrow about my devastated country, my suffering people, the Turkish leaders who continue to depict me as a separatist and traitor, simply because I have a different conception of my country's future and of the happiness of the Kurdish and Turkish peoples.

Your prize shows that beyond differences of language, religion, and race, women and men of good will who want peace can come together around the universal values of human rights and democracy. I am glad to be a member of that universal family. And on 4 November, in my prison in Ankara, I will be thinking of all of you. I am with you in my heart, my spiritual sisters and brothers, and I now also feel that I am a little bit Norwegian.

Thank you again for your solidarity and friendship.

With all my respect and my warmest greetings.

Letter to Kendal Nezan

Exiled Kurdish intellectual from Turkey
Founder and president of the Kurdish Institute of Paris (1983)

22 October 1994

My dear friend:

After the spring comes the summer. Here is yet another season that I am spending in the shadows, deep inside a jail. I cannot see the sky, but it must be full of large black clouds, for I hear the rain beating down. It must be a typical fall day, the kind that makes you melancholy. I am listening to one of Sivan's[1] tapes, and the good-bye party you threw for us in Paris passes before my eyes like a movie. It was so good of Sivan to come to Paris just for our party. With the intuition of an artist, he must have guessed he would not see us again for many years.

My favorite season is springtime. Especially April and May, when we witness the miracle of nature's renewal. In a few days, the countryside will be covered with a bed of daisies, poppies, daffodils, crocuses, and hyacinths, a thousand and one flowers that it would take pages simply to list. Narcissuses grow at the edge of springs, trees are in flower, lilacs and roses perfume the air, and the sheep are bearing their young. The chirping of the birds and the tender bleating of the lambs enchant the ears. I wish I were a musician or a painter and could compose a pastoral symphony or paint the dawn of spring in the village where I spent my childhood and youth. I don't know if city people like you feel the same way about nature and the change of seasons. You will nonetheless agree with me, I hope, that springtime in Kurdistan is magnificent.

All this goes to say that I have suffered from being shut up during my favorite season. I could bear several years in prison if every year they let me out in April and May for a sort of seasonal holiday or break from persecution. Obviously, I know that in the real world, particularly in our country, heir to centuries of despotism and where the life and hopes of a man or woman don't count, this is pure fantasy. I notice in fact that recently I am more likely to give in to revery. Sometimes I am in the Kurdish mountains, free as a bird, sometimes in the teeming crowds of Diyarbakir, amidst my people, surrounded with affection and warmth; sometimes in the streets of Paris, my favorite European city, which I love so much. My jailers have locked up my body, but as you see, my spirit does not know bars, nor prohibitions, nor borders.

Is this the result of my long detention and isolation? Is it the melancholy air of fall? I don't know. Maybe it's a way of escaping the boredom of prison days, which seem to be all the same. The only change is the change of guards, every six hours. Reading, writing, and music allow me to fill up my time and vary the long monotony a little. I also try to get a little physical exercise and to study French. I miss daylight and space very much. My only real moments of relaxation are the family and lawyers' visits. They allow me to emerge from my isolation and talk with friends, other imprisoned members of Parliament, visitors, and lawyers, who make all kinds of jokes. We laugh a lot together and make fun of everything and everyone, beginning with ourselves. Mehdi,[2] who has so much experience in Turkish prisons, also manages to lift everyone's spirits. You know he has a sense of humor under any circumstances.

I am not sad or discouraged, and certainly not beaten down. I know you must be worried about my health. I would like to be able to reassure you on that score. But in spite of all my efforts, it is just not that great. It has even gotten worse in the last three months. I have constant pain in my bones. I often feel chilled even though I'm running a fever. I don't understand it, and the doctors don't seem to, either.

They were supposed to hospitalize me on October 4, but they didn't. I think those idiots are afraid I will escape! Whenever they bring me to the hospital, they take security measures as extraordinary as they are ridiculous to prevent the possibility of escape. Last time, my doctor at the hospital told his prison colleague that my condition required regular follow-up treatment at the hospital, and that if a period of hospitalization was not possible, then they should bring me to the hospital regularly for checkups. But on the order of the government or the prosecutor of the State Security Court, my medical visits have been limited to a strict minimum, for fear of an escape. I make fun of them, saying:

"Even if you left the doors wide open, I would not leave because I am not that stupid. I am here in the name of a cause, for having defended a certain idea of law, democracy and justice. By putting me in prison you have given my cause publicity and have attracted the attention of world public opinion to my people's fate. Thanks to your blunders, the whole world now knows the Kurdish tragedy in Turkey. For me it is an honor to have contributed to this awareness. I will leave prison only when the court of public conscience and justice has recognized that my cause is just. All these security measure are thus unnecessary!"

To close this chapter on the hospital, I learned the other day that the results of lab tests done weeks ago have been lost! In this police world, corrupted by negligence and lies, everyone tries to lay the blame on someone else. I'll have to do them over again! It is a strange country where men, who are arrested or kidnapped in broad daylight, disappear without a trace, without it being possible to find out who is responsible for the disappearance. How, then, given such conditions, could one hope to find out who is responsible for the loss of a medical file? Nothing is worth less than a human life in this country. The life of a Kurd, even a member of Parliament, is worth less than Mumtaz Soysal's[3] cat or Nusret Demiral's[4] dog.

We are preparing for the next hearings. Since the trial is truly a travesty of justice, its outcome depends on the degree of international pressure. The verdict could be handed down within the next few weeks, and we are calm, ready for any eventuality, including the scaffold. We know that in the recent past, on the basis of charges made up out of whole cloth, the military was able to send a civilian prime minister and several of his innocent ministers[5] to the gallows, and that after the March 1971 coup d'état, Deniz Gezmis and his equally innocent friends were hung by the military as part of their traditional policy of terrorizing civilian society. Every month Kurdish civilians, democrats, and innocents, including lawyers, doctors, and human rights activists, are assassinated by the death squads of the Turkish police, while others "disappear" in police stations and torture centers. I think of Musa Anter, Mehmet Sincar, Medet Serhat, Yusuf Ekinci, Vedat Aydin[6] and so many others. My blood is no redder than theirs.

And then, as the proverb says: "It is the jug's destiny to break on the way to the spring one day." But I will fight to the end.

Our destiny will be decided by the generals through the National Security Council, which they control. The Court will be responsible for finding legal window dressing for the judgment. We have no illusions about this. In political cases like this one, the judges are simply notaries who stamp their seal on decisions dictated to them by the army, based on power relations. Since domestic public opinion does not count, it is only international public opinion, particularly pressure from Western governments, that could ultimately influence their decisions.

We must realize that the Turkish leaders are very deft in diplomacy and in the manipulation of public opinion. Heirs of a centuries-long tradition of Byzantine and Ottoman intrigue and ruse, they know how to fool people and how to create illusions. Not to mention the peasant naiveté of the Kurds, who have so often been fooled and manipulated by Turkish chiefs with promises that are never fulfilled. And the Turkish state has skillfully managed to fool the Western world as well. For sixty-six years the leaders' policy has been based on lies. In the 1920s and 1930s, during Atatürk's one-party rule, they massacred and deported Kurds, justifying their acts by "the struggle against feudalism and religious reaction" and by presenting themselves as "secular progressives." During World War II, they flirted with both Germany and the Allies. After the war, seeing which way the wind was blowing, they adopted a multiparty façade, though preventing all political expression on the part of the Kurds, as well as of the workers and leftist movements. The struggle against the communist peril became the inexhaustible stock in trade of the Turkish regime, from whom the Western allies accepted anything, including the bloody coups d'état and the crushing of the Kurdish people, in the name of that "strategic imperative." Since this advantage has come to an end with the fall of Communism, they are now brandishing the specter of Islamic fundamentalism, and they say: "If you don't help us, Turkey will fall into the Islamist camp." At the same time, the state is doing whatever it can to encourage the development of the Islamist Welfare Party [RP] in the Kurdish regions, as a way of opposing the Kurdish democratic movement.

If you remember, in last March's [1994] municipal elections the Army Chief of Staff asked all the other parties to withdraw from the Kurdish regions and give the advantage to the Welfare Party [RP] in order to block "the separatists." Knowing that after Communism, Islamic fundamentalism has become the ideological enemy of the Americans, our leaders are helping the Islamist party increase its power and then using that increase in power to present themselves as a rampart against Islamic fundamentalism, all in order to obtain financial and military aid from the Americans and other Western powers! The worst thing is that this gross ruse seems to work. The Turkish leaders manage to manipulate and fool their Western allies. On the pretext of a struggle against the Islamic peril and terrorism, they win the indulgence and support of their allies for the worst exactions. They even succeed in convincing them that the democratization of the country's structures will be carried out once these dangers have been eliminated. And this same old song, regularly trotted out for a half a century, or in any case since the formation of the current DYP-SHP [True Path Party and Social Democrat Populist Party] government coalition in November 1991, still seems to work in creating illusions.

I can't understand how the Western powers, with their intelligent, educated, and lucid leaders, let themselves be fooled in this way, unless their spirit and judgment are clouded by commercial interests, which rank higher than the interests of people who defend freedom and human rights.

Having gotten to this point in a letter that has become very long, I ask myself why I am writing to you about things that you know as well as, if not better than, I do. I probably need to express my feelings. To write, to exchange, is a pleasant escape, a way of escaping from the isolation of my cell. And then, who knows when I will have the chance to write again and to find a way of getting a letter to you.

Write me as often as you can, to give me news of the outside world, our friends, and my children, whom I miss a lot. I hope they aren't causing you any problems and that you can spare them some time to keep an eye on their school work. I also count on you to give my regards and my best wishes for his health to President [François] Mitterrand, and to express our gratitude to Mme.

[Danielle] Mitterrand for her generous and precious action on our behalf. Cordial greetings also to Ségolène Royal, Antoinette Fouque, and Sylvie Jan, who have proved that solidarity among women truly exists and can encourage women in the third world to involve themselves actively in the struggle for their emancipation and for democracy. Don't forget to send my greetings and gratitude to the lawyers of the collective that took up our defense. Give my greetings to all those who are kind enough to ask about me.

Affectionately,

1. Sivan Perwer is a popular Kurdish singer who lives in exile in Sweden.
2. Leyla Zana's husband, Mehdi Zana, former mayor of Diyarbakir, spent more than fifteen years in Turkish prisons for his opinions. When this letter was written, he was serving a four-year sentence as a result of his 1992 testimony before the European Parliament (he was released in December 1995). He has written several books in Kurdish and Turkish, one of which, on torture in the prison of Diyarbakir, has been published in English as *Prison No. 5: Eleven Years in Turkish Jails.* Watertown, MA: Blue Crane Books, 1997; preface by Elie Wiesel. Today, he lives in exile.
3. Turkish Minister of Foreign Affairs at the time, known for his extreme nationalism, his defense of the authors of the putsch against Gorbachev, and his sympathy for Saddam Hussein in the name of "anti-imperialism."
4. Far-right prosecutor of the State Security Court in Ankara. One of the key figures in the legal system set up by the 1980 military junta, this prosecutor, known for demanding the death sentence for people convicted for their opinions, has publicly boasted of "loving Hitler as he does dogs." He has composed an elegy to his dog.
5. This refers to Adnan Menderes and two ministers of the Democracy Party [DEP]; they were sentenced to death by the authors of the 1960 military coup d'état.
6. Famous Kurdish poet and writer, Musa Anter was assassinated on 20 September 1992 near Diyarbakir. Mehmet Sincar, Democracy Party [DEP] member of Parliament from Mardin, was assassinated on 4 September 1993 at Batman in an attack that also targeted Leyla Zana. Medet Serhat, and Yusuf Ekinci, two pacifist lawyers known to be Kurdish patriots, were assassinated in 1994, the former in Istanbul and the latter in Ankara, by the Turkish antiguerrilla warfare units. Vedat Aydin, president of the Diyarbakir chapter of the Association for Human Rights before becoming president of the Diyarbakir Federation of the HEP [Peoples' Labor Party], precursor to the Democracy Party [DEP], was kidnapped by the police from his home in Diyarbakir; his corpse was found on 8 July 1991 at the side of a road.

Letter to Antoinette Fouque
President of the Women's Alliance for Democracy,
Member of the European Parliament

30 November 1994

Dear Antoinette Fouque:

Many thanks for the interest and solidarity you have shown me, and through me, for all Kurdish women. I send you my greetings with affection and respect.

I was very happy that you were at the 10 November hearing and am so sorry I was unable to see you. My mother had a lot to tell me about you. She said: "Daughter, as long as we have friends like that, nothing else matters." She is so glad to have met you. When she talked about you, her eyes shone. I think that my mother is more worried about my children than about me. When I ask her how they are, she starts to cry. Like every oppressed Kurdish woman, my mother has suffered a great deal and has lived through very difficult times. But through her ordeals she learned the value of freedom. Ten years ago, the Kurdish people in general, and Kurdish women in particular, lived in conditions of slavery. The women bore their unhappiness fatalistically, saying: "Such is our destiny." But for the last few years, with the development of the struggle for freedom, women have evolved and gone through rapid transformation. Kurdish women have gotten to this level by paying a heavy price for freedom. In Lice in 1990, Kudret Filiz, a forty-eight-year-old mother, lead a popular uprising. The price she paid for freedom was being run over by a tank. Such women serve as examples, for by their sacrifice they help us see our own condition more clearly, and they give us courage.

They have shown by their actions that women are human beings and must live a human life, but that this will not come about without a struggle.

Even today, it is women who suffer the most and who shed most of the tears. Every day they are traumatized by the death of the children they have raised with so much effort and such difficulty. The children of poor Turkish people are sent into this area and also lose their lives in this dirty war. We note that it is the Kurdish and Turkish women who pay the consequences of the social, political, and economic crises caused by this war.

The fact that those in power want to solve the Kurdish problem by continuing the war and do not envisage a peaceful settlement is making everything increasingly difficult. The reason that we are behind bars, enclosed within concrete walls, is that we became aware of these problems early on, and we have proposed a peaceful solution that is within the context of democracy and the equality of our two peoples. Contrary to what they claim, we have emphasized egalitarian coexistence more than separation. Obviously, that position contradicts the policy of the charlatans who defend the war. We were thrown out of Parliament in a way that has no precedent in the world and that violates every standard of law, and we were sent to prison.

Through us, those in power aim to intimidate the Kurdish people and the democratic forces of Turkey and to terrorize and silence the whole society.

Government policy is leading Turkey toward exclusion from the international community. I sincerely believe that the Turkish people do not deserve this. It is the government that bears the whole responsibility.

I think that few peoples in the world suffer more than the Kurdish and Turkish people are suffering now. At a time when the world is being globalized, the trials inflicted on our peoples should be a shame for all humanity. We live at a time when the history and identity of a people are still being negated and its culture destroyed. On this subject, I think that women, who have always contributed to world peace, have much to do.

I was glad to see Taslima Nasrin courageously demand a new interpretation of the Koran. I congratulate her through you and greet her with affection and respect. In the case of Iran, all women can now see the state to which Moslem countries reduce them by an exclusively male interpretation of the Koran. The fact that Taslima Nasrin has won a prize[1] is a fitting acknowledgment of women, of the fact that they, too are human beings, and, as such, must be free.

I have also written to M. [François] Mitterrand. I ask you to please give him my regards.

The state of my health, which was never very good, has gotten worse in the primitive living conditions of the prison, which does poor health like mine no good.

Unfortunately, I have not seen the sun in summer or fall. Daylight does not enter the courtyard where I take my walks. The courtyard measures only three meters by ten, which prevents me from seeing the sky. I can have family visits once a week, for two hours, behind a double glass and bars. I cannot meet the other parliamentarians who are in prison with me, except when our lawyers come to see us. In sum, I am alone with two guards who watch me. I have no problem with them. In fact, I think that there are no problems between peoples. If governments would provide the leadership, people would live in fraternal peace without distinction of race, language, or religion, and without tears or suffering.

Wishing you success in your projects, I embrace you and assure you of my affection and respect.

1. The 1994 Sakharov Prize for Freedom of Thought.

Letter to Pauline Green
President of the Socialist Group of the European Parliament

13 December 1994

Dear Madam:

As you know, the State Security Court [DGM] has convicted my colleagues and myself, after six hearings, without heeding the defense lawyers' requests, without cross-examination of prosecution witnesses, without producing the originals of the wiretap recordings they claim to have, and without carrying out the necessary investigations—in sum, without respecting the universal rules of law and of a fair trial. We are sure that our conviction was decided on by the National Security Council [MGK], which is dominated by the military. The role of the State Security Court was merely to find the appropriate legal window dressing for the National Security Council's decision. Our only crimes are defending democracy and peace in Turkey and bearing witness to the realities the people are living.

We want you to know that it was only due to international pressure that we were not given the death sentence, and that the Court, in order to give the impression of being just, gave us different sentences.

Keeping up the pressure will contribute to the democratization of Turkey. Your efforts support the struggle of the democratic forces in Turkey for a democracy compatible with universal values and standards.

Even if I were permanently stripped of my freedom, I would continue the peaceful struggle for human rights and democracy that I have been carrying out for the last fourteen years. My health permitting, I will continue to shout out our aspirations for peace and democracy.

With best regards.

Leyla Zana

Letter to Miguel Angel Martinez

President of the Parliamentary Assembly of
the Council of Europe

12 January 1995

Mr. President:

We would like to express our gratitude for the interest that the Council of Europe has shown us since our parliamentary immunity was lifted on 2 March 1994.

We realize that this interest stems from your concerns not only for us personally, but also for the destiny of the Kurdish people, whom we represent, and for the future of democracy and internal peace in Turkey. You hope that in such an unstable region, Turkey (which you consider part of Europe) will have a secular, democratic government, be a stable, strong ally, respectful of human rights and universal standards of pluralistic democracy, and become a respectable member of the community of Western nations. Through constructive criticism, you have made many efforts in this direction.

But unfortunately, the forces that lead our country continue to govern by a Constitution and laws imposed by the 1980 military coup d'état and by institutions like the State Security Court [DGM] and the National Security Council [MGK], which are incompatible with a just state and the free expression of the will of the people. The so-called democratic reforms that these groups have promised since 1991 have never gotten beyond the stage of flash announcements and declarations of intent destined to fool public opinion. These groups have not taken even the smallest step toward a democratic and peaceful settlement of the Kurdish question, which is the country's basic problem. The process of dialogue that [former president] Mr. Turgut Özal wanted to initiate has been dropped; and by negating the very existence of the Kurdish problem, government leaders have returned to the fanatic Turkish nationalism of the 1930s. The lack of a solution has led Turkey to the greatest social, political, economic, and moral crisis of its history.

It is within this context that our trial must be understood. In fact, the trial has revealed to the general public what the Turkish political and legal system really is. It has thus been transformed into a trial of that system.

In sum, on 3 August, after five months of detention (which had been decided by a prosecutor of the State Security Court without a judge's opinion), we were sent to Court. On the basis of fabricated, imaginary allegations and without permitting cross-examination of prosecution witnesses, without playing wiretap recordings that were supposed to contain criminal evidence nor permitting independent experts to examine them, rejecting as a block nearly fifty requests to call witnesses and investigative and expert testimony presented by our lawyers, the Court, in six hearings, sentenced five members of Parliament to fifteen years, one to seven-years, and two others to three-years in prison. We had said beforehand that the sentences were decided on by the National Security Council, dominated by the military, which is the *de facto* government of the country, and that the role of the State Security Court was merely to find an article of the penal code corresponding to these sentences in order to give them some legal window dressing. Moreover, during the last hearing, the Court announced that it was dropping the accusations on which the trial had been based so far and would be trying us on a new accusation (i.e., links to the PKK [Kurdistan Workers' Party]). We leave it to you to decide to what extent this comedy, played out before Western observers and the press, is compatible with law and with the principle of a fair trial.

A few weeks later, the same State Security Court handed down fifteen-year prison terms to some Islamist prisoners who were tried for having burned alive thirty-seven left-wing intellectuals and artists in a hotel in Sivas. Thus, in Turkey, members of Parliament, on the one hand guilty of peacefully expressing the demands and hopes of their constituents and charged simply because of their opinions, and on the other hand, fanatics who, in broad daylight and in full view of the security forces, burn alive intellectuals and artists participating in a cultural festival, receive the same prison sentences.

To become definitive, our sentences must be confirmed by the Court of Appeals. Our lawyers have appealed. The public prosecutor of the State Security Court has also appealed, again demanding the death sentence. Normally, the Court of Appeals would be unlikely to overturn the State Security Court's verdict and decide to free us, because of the judges' well-known extreme nationalistic tendencies and because most of the judges were appointed under the military regime and are thus linked to the military milieu. Only intense international pressure could bring the leaders of the Turkish Republic to choose to overturn the verdict.

As you know, although our sentences have not yet been confirmed, six of us remain incarcerated. Furthermore, our party [the Democracy Party, DEP] was outlawed on 16 June 1994 by the Constitutional Court on the pretext of "separatist propaganda" attributed to our former president and to a peace appeal our party made. Thus, on the bases of a crime of opinion and of collective guilt, both of which are unacceptable in a civilized legal system, thirteen freely elected members of Parliament have been stripped of their mandates. Following this legal scandal, which no democratic conscience would accept, the people of Kurdish provinces including Diyarbakir, Batman, Mardin, Sirnak, Siirt, Adiyaman, and Van are no longer represented in the Turkish Parliament. By the same token the results of outlawing the Democracy Party, which expressed the aspirations and opinions of an important sector of the Kurdish people of Turkey, and of defending their views in democratic, peaceful ways, are the silencing and removal from Parliament of a political tendency that has an important and unique place in the political spectrum of the country. For these two basic reasons, it is obvious that the Turkish Parliament does not represent all of Turkey's citizens, nor does it reflect the will of the people fully and fairly. Now even the president of the Parliament, Mr. Cindoruk, admits that Parliament is not democratic. In particular, in the climate of intellectual and physical terrorism created by the arrest of the Democracy Party parliamentarians, the Parliament has become an organization dominated by fear, reduced to swallowing directives from the National Security Council.

We think it would be useful to bring to your attention two cases that epitomize this serious development. Last October [1994], the policy of the army's evacuating and burning down Kurdish villages and depopulating the region was intensified in the province of Tunceli (Dersim). In just a few weeks, you could see the destruction of tens of Kurdish villages and the forced exodus of peasants, victims of this disaster. Mr. A. Köylüoglu, minister of Human Rights elected from this province, after investigating the case mainly by listening to the victims, had the courage to say that the destruction of the villages was the work of the state and that the security forces practiced state terrorism in that region. But the prime minister, the military commanders, and ministers acting as their spokesmen asserted: "The state could not burn down its own villages; that was done by terrorists disguised as soldiers." In answer to this question by some mayor : "How could terrorists attack by helicopter?" the prime minister declared that he "had proof that the PKK came from Armenia and Russia aboard helicopters." Thus, the prime minister, who boasts every day of having "eradicated terrorism," claims that the PKK, which the government considers a terrorist organization, could have carried out a helicopter attack on the province of Tunceli, located some three or four hundred kilometers from the nearest border, and burned down villages, despite the presence of hundreds of thousands of Turkish soldiers in the area. The fact that such allegations are considered normal propaganda and disinformation gives one food for thought about the dreadful level to which political debate in the country has been reduced.

To calm the debates about the destruction of Kurdish villages, the Parliament decided to create an investigative commission . But even though three months have passed, the commission's requests have gone unmet. The military authorities in the region have not permitted the parliamentary commission to enter and carry out their investigation.

The second case is that of assassinations in which the perpetrators have not been identified; this issue remains an open wound in Turkey. According to the newspaper *Milliyet* of 11 December 1994 in the past two years 3,840 civilians have been assassinated by unidentified killers or have died as a result of non legal executions or under torture. More than a year ago, a parliamentary Commission was created to investigate the forces who commit these murders and their aims. But institutions like the army, the police, the intelligence agency [MIT], and the Ministry of the Interior would not cooperate with the Commission, and its work was a total fiasco. Contrary to the custom in democratic countries, in Turkey the Parliament, which theoretically represents the will of the people, is considered insignificant by the forces that control the country, and therefore it cannot carry out its function of checking the executive body.

Today, we are behind bars because we wanted, despite the censure and prohibitions of the centers of illegitimate, nonelected power, to accomplish our duty as elected representatives, to express our constituents' grievances, and to serve the causes of internal peace and democracy. For trying to shed light on events like the annihilation of the Kurdish elite (among whom eighty-four leaders and directors of our party have been assassinated by unidentified killers), the evacuation and destruction of Kurdish villages, the bombing of our forests, the forced exodus of the Kurdish population on the pretext of the fight against terrorism, the Turkish leaders want to silence us to prevent us from letting the public know the tragedy that the Kurdish people are living.

For the same reasons, Ankara has not permitted observers from the Conference on Security and Cooperation in Europe [CSCE] to go to the Kurdish regions and has severely limited the press's ability to disperse information.

It is very difficult to grasp the realities or to understand the impasse in which the country finds itself simply by looking at showcase cities like Istanbul and Ankara. One must visit Diyarbakir and the surrounding area, however briefly, in order to see what President [Süleyman] Demirel himself called the country's number one problem, "the problem of the Southeast"—that is to say, the tragic Kurdish reality. If not, Turkish diplomacy knows how to appease foreigners visiting Ankara with little time to spare by offering nice but hollow promises of "democratic reforms soon to be placed on the agenda." During such visits, the diplomats first call an emergency meeting of a "human rights" or "democratization" committee or commission. After the visits no one ever again mentions the existence of these commissions. Then the leaders use parliamentary arithmetic to explain the fact that the promises made were never realized. But when necessary, or when the National Security Council orders it, they can get a parliamentary majority vote in two days, as was seen when the immunity of the Democracy Party parliamentarians was lifted.

We read in the newspapers that during the visit of the Council of Europe delegation to Turkey, the government again made a series of promises about democratization. It is unfortunately clear that during these four months no step has been taken either toward democratization or toward a search for a peaceful settlement of the Kurdish problem by means of dialogue. Since coming to power in November 1991, the coalition government formed by the True Path Party [DYP] and Social Democrat Populist Party [SHP] has made many promises of this nature. That is why we also supported the coalition in its first few months, but after the massacre of more than one hundred Kurdish civilians during the 1992 *Nevruz*[1] festivities, we were compelled to question the sincerity and seriousness of these promises.

Our heavy prison sentences, the arrests of writers, journalists, and intellectuals every day, and the tragic extent of the persecution inflicted on the Kurdish people reveal Turkey's true policy. The evidence points not to an improvement in the situation, but to a grave deterioration.

The response of world public opinion to the sentences we were given, in particular the resolution taken by the European Parliament,[2] the decision of the European Union to postpone the signing of a Customs Treaty with Turkey and to demand our freedom have again placed the debate on "democratization" on the agenda, but there is still no concrete progress. We expect that before the meeting of your Council these promises will be renewed; but without intense external pressure, they are unlikely to be realized.

We read in the press that the issue of Turkey's membership is to be discussed at the next meeting of the Council of Europe's Parliamentary Assembly, and that some countries are also considering raising the issue at the meeting of the Council's Committee of Ministers. The Turkish officials have given you their views, and we expect them to send a strong delegation to your meeting as well. But we Kurdish parliamentarians who have been kept behind bars for eleven months even though we were elected by the Kurdish people, consider it an obligation flowing from the mission our people have entrusted us with to write you this long letter in order to let you know our point of view and our situation and to supplement your information.

It is for you to decide to what extent Turkey's current practices and its Constitution and laws are compatible with the principles and rules of your Council and with your concepts of democracy, human rights, civil liberties, and the rights and prerogatives of a Parliament and its members. It is our most cherished wish that one day Turkey will become a truly pluralistic, secular democracy, one that recognizes the political and cultural diversity of its people, is secure in internal peace and stability, and is respectful of universal standards of human rights and democracy. We will continue to struggle with all our might, by peaceful means, for that Turkey, where the Kurdish and Turkish peoples can live as brothers in equality, peace, and democracy. We believe that a truly democratic Turkey will have a respectable place in the European Community. The greatest support that European democrats can give us now would be to refuse to sacrifice the high principles of democracy to the interests of Realpolitik.

In this hope, we offer you our deepest respect.

In the name of the Kurdish members of Parliament imprisoned in the Ankara Central Prison.

Leyla Zana
Member of Parliament from Diyarbakir

1. Traditional Kurdish New Year, celebrated on March 21.
2. The European Parliament adopted a resolution that "denounces the attack on pluralist democracy by the Turkish government"; "requests the immediate release" of the Kurdish members of Parliament in question "whose only crime is to have defended the interests of the Kurdish people in Turkey who are the victims of brutal military repression"; "calls once again on the Turkish government finally to recognize the right of autonomy of the Kurdish people in Turkey"; and "to revoke the decision lifting their parliamentary immunity so that they can once more enjoy their constitutional rights." (*European Parliament Press Review*, 9 March 1994)

Letter to Sylvie Jan
President of the International Democratic Federation of Women

7 March 1995

My dear Sylvie:

I received your message of solidarity, which made me very happy. Through our lawyers and the press we know about the demonstrations you are organizing to demand my release from prison and, through me, the release of all my imprisoned colleagues. We have also been receiving messages of solidarity from women of many countries. I very much appreciate the efforts your Federation is making and the effectiveness of those efforts. I thank you with all my heart and want to express my deep gratitude to you.

In spite of the difficult prison conditions, I try my best to make my contribution to the struggle for peace and democracy. Whenever I can, I give statements to the local and international press. In the past few months I have received increasing support from the Turkish public, particularly from women. In the appeal I wrote for International Women's Day on 8 March, I asked the women of Turkey to organize themselves to struggle for peace and democracy, to say no to war and violence, and to begin, through dialogue, to seek civilized, democratic solutions to the problems of the country, especially the Kurdish problem. The fact that Turkish women are finally beginning to understand us bodes well for the future. I believe that together we can prepare a better and freer future for our children. We will never forget your contribution to this struggle. I think that the struggle that we are waging in such difficult conditions also contributes to the struggle of women everywhere for equality, peace, and democracy. And despite prison conditions, despite my health, which remains poor because I do not get adequate treatment, I am determined to continue to fight to the end.

I thank you again for your support and your solidarity and embrace you affectionately.

Letter to François Mitterrand
President of France

4 May 1995

M. President:

The letter that you were kind enough to send me[1] made me and my fellow prisoners very happy. The fact that France and the other nations of the European Union are willing to follow our problems so closely is strong support for us and for the struggle for democracy we are waging. We know what our struggle owes to your personal concern and to the efforts of France, the country that gave world civilization the Declaration of Human Rights.

We are all very touched that in the last days of your term, with your heavy responsibilities, you thought of us and, through us, of the fate of the Turkish and Kurdish peoples. We thank you immensely and will never forget your concern and the many ways in which you have helped us.

There is still no change in our situation. Our lawyers have indeed appealed to the Court of Appeals, but we have still received no answer, either positive or negative.

None of the democratic reforms that the Turkish government have repeatedly promised—most recently at the signing of the Customs Union Treaty—and that are essential for all the people of Turkey have yet been realized.

Even the president of the Turkish Republic, Mr. Süleyman Demirel, speaking about the proposed amelioration of Article 8 of the antiterrorist law, which restricts freedom of expression under any conditions, declared: "That the military must be consulted first." He thus dismissed the principle of the separation of legislative, executive, and judicial powers, which is the law in democratic countries. That seems unacceptable to us.

Unfortunately, we still see no progress in the areas of internal peace and the free expression of "Kurdish identity," which Mr. Demirel publicly recognized in 1991.

We are concerned that these leaders' incoherent, contradictory statements have made Turkey appear unreliable in the eyes of domestic and international public opinion. What is even more depressing is that they are leading the country toward an economic and moral crisis and, in fact, toward an increasingly more serious political crisis.

We express our opinions and concerns to the Western friends and fellow parliamentarians who come to see us, and we repeat our belief that internal peace and stability in Turkey will be achieved only through a peaceful, truly democratic settlement of the Kurdish question.

We hope that Turkey will overcome its fear that "Europe wants to divide Turkey" and will come to trust its Western allies, and that the allies will act in concert to support the country's democratic forces.

We will continue to struggle to end the bloodshed between brothers, to confront the difficulties ahead of us, and to support all struggle for democracy, social compromise, and internal peace.

We continue to hope that the leaders of the Western democracies, whom you have interested in our cause and who, thanks to you, have supported us, will, in the name of the common interests of our countries, and of the defense of democracy, peace, and stability in the region, continue to offer their support.

Please accept our profound thanks and gratitude for the support that you have unceasingly offered our people and for the interest and friendship you have shown me and my imprisoned fellow parliamentarians, as well as our best wishes for your health, our respect and our affection. Our regards and affectionate greetings to your most admirable wife.

Leyla Zana
Ankara Central Prison

1. See the letter of 24 April 1995 on page xv.

Message to the World Conference on Women in Beijing

25 August 1995

How I would have loved to participate in the Conference, to meet women from all over the world, to learn from their ideas and testimony, and to testify myself about the unenviable fate of women in my country.

Sentenced to fifteen years in prison for words and actions on behalf of democracy and peace, I and five of my colleagues have spent the past eighteen months behind the bars of Ankara Central Prison.

I assume that the Turkish delegates, unhampered by embarrassing witnesses like me, will give the usual version of official ideology—that is, that Turkey is the only secular state in the Moslem world whose laws grant equal rights to women, that it is also headed by a woman prime minister, and that women hold many important positions in all sectors of society. In sum, everything is about on the same level as in the Western nations.

Like all authoritarian regimes, the Turkish government presents a good facade. On paper, everything was almost perfect in the Shah's Iran and in Saddam Hussein's Iraq, too, where women who served merely as figureheads and who were exhibited in the regime's showcase window were meant to demonstrate progress in women's status.

But the reality, alas, is otherwise. One need only look at the Report on Humanitarian Development recently published by the United Nations, in which Turkey ranks 98th of 115 countries in women's participation in economic and political life. In this country, dominated by centuries of military, macho, despotic, and Moslem traditions, women's voices can barely be heard. Of the 450 seats in the National Assembly, we were only 8 women. I was the only Kurdish woman parliamentarian in a country of sixty million people, including about eithteen million Kurds. I refused to accept a merely decorative role and decided to speak up in Parliament about the people's problems and suffering, including questions hitherto considered taboo—like the army's destruction of the Kurdish countryside, the forced uprooting of people, and the assassination of democrats by death squads. The generals, who wield most of the power in Turkey through the National Security Council, decided to punish me, first by two assassination attempts, and then by throwing me into prison. It is the usual command: Woman, shut up!

In this remarkable Turkish democracy, a inister of state has kept his position even though he publicly described as "prostitutes" three eminent women members of the European Parliament—the presidents of the Socialist, Radical, and Green groups, who were guilty of being concerned about my fate and about the human rights situation in the country. And a Turkish parliamentarian who publicly struck and injured an airline stewardess who had asked him not to take his revolver aboard was not even prosecuted, since such aggression is commonplace. This parliamentarian is protected by parliamentary immunity, just like another accused of sexual harassment and like 152 others accused of various crimes such as embezzlement, corruption, and fraudulent bankruptcy. Only my Kurdish colleagues of the Democracy Party and I, guilty of expressing nonconformist opinions, have been brought to trial, convicted, and imprisoned.

I know that nowhere in the world do women yet enjoy true equality. But the situation is particularly serious for women in the Moslem world. Polygamy, seclusion, repudiation, forced marriage, difficult access to education and employment, and major obstacles to participation in public life are the common lot of Moslem women, even in those countries whose laws theoretically recognize the equality of the sexes. In countries such as Turkey, Iran, Iraq, or Algeria, where overt or covert wars are being waged, with their train of destruction, forced uprooting and poverty, women, mothers, are crushed by the weight of their responsibilities. In my country, an undeclared war has been waged for more than ten years. The army has evacuated and destroyed more than three thousand Kurdish villages, bombed and burned mountains and forests, and forced nearly three million innocent Kurdish peasants off their ancestral land, leaving them to sink into poverty.

The dead, wounded, and disabled number in the tens of thousands. Women like me who want the right to teach their mother tongue to their children freely and who seek to express Kurdish identity and culture within a democratic framework are considered terrorists and are persecuted.

While being a woman is difficult in many countries, being a women, Moslem and Kurd in a country like Turkey is a kind of martyrdom.

But here as elsewhere women are fighting to change the destiny that others are trying to impose on them and to achieve a genuine equality between the sexes. Such equality is not only a moral requirement but is also the indispensable condition for the development of society, for the progress of democracy, and for culture to blossom. Women's fight for equal rights is essentially a humanist and peaceful struggle for true democracy, and a higher form of civilization.

I hope that the Beijing Conference, through its debates and resolutions, will make an important advance in our struggle. I fervently hope for its success and send warm greetings to all the participants.

Leyla Zana
Ankara Central Prison

Message on Being Awarded the International Peace Prize of Aix-la-Chapelle

30 August 1995

Dear Friends:

Although I am unable to participate personally in the 1 September Peace Day ceremonies and activities organized by the Aix-la-Chapelle Association for the Peace Prize, I want you to know that I am with you in spirit and extend my greetings to you with affection and respect.

Aside from the meaning that Peace Day always has, the fact that 1995 is "the year of tolerance" gives this particular Peace Day an even deeper significance.

Peace, for which this day is named, is an aspiration, an action, and an indispensable way of life. Like freedom, it is won only through great effort and intense sacrifice and preserved only through discipline and tolerance. It is nourished by love, and as long as it is nourished, it reigns and thrives.

Peace is a necessary condition of life. We cherish it particularly ever since the two World Wars, which caused suffering that is still vivid in our minds, and we shiver with fear at the thought of them. But unfortunately, peace does not yet prevail everywhere in the world.

In spite of the steadily growing level of organization of the pacifist movements, which are opposed to war, open or covert wars are still being waged today in Bosnia, Chechnya, Algeria, Turkey, Iraq, Kurdistan, and many other places. I am convinced that these wars do not concern only the Bosnians, Chechens, Russians, Serbs, Turks, and Kurds. In some way they concern all humanity, and they are shaping its present and future as well as its entire system of values.

The tragedy of hundreds of thousands of Bosnians evicted from their cities and towns in the name of ethnic cleansing is a barbaric denial of the universal values of civilization that have evolved with such difficulty. The fact that in Algeria and Iran they are trying, in the name of religion, to throw the whole society, and particularly the women, back into the darkness of the Middle Ages is a great threat to everyone's freedom, whether man or woman, Moslem, Christian, or secular. In my country, the fact that the state, in the name of a fanatic nationalism and on the pretext of fighting terrorism, has evacuated and destroyed more than three thousand Kurdish villages, set fire to our mountains and burned down our forests, forced millions of innocent Kurdish peasants to leave their region and their lands and, torn up by the roots, to sink into poverty, and destroyed my people's traditional way of life, economy, and culture that evolved through thousands of years of close contact with nature is a tragedy not only for the Kurds, but also for all humanity. It is a true moral, political, economic, and ecological disaster.

I am sure that anyone, whatever his language, color, or religious belief, who supports humanist values and the rights of man and nature, and who believes as I do that humanity is one, experiences any injustice toward a person or a people as an injustice committed against all of humanity and has the clear awareness that nature, beyond the divisions of language and race, is the common property and heritage of all people. That is why the democrats, pacifists, and ecologists cannot and must not remain silent in face of a nameless war carried out for more than ten years in a corner of our common motherland, the Earth. This is dirty, bloody war in which Kurds and Turks die every day, afflicting Turkish and Kurdish mothers and sowing the seeds of hatred between the two peoples.

We must join forces to silence the weapons, end war and violence, and create a climate in which people can work out solutions to their problems within the framework of democracy by means of dialogue, debate, and compromise.

In spite of the fact that in the seventy-two years of the Turkish Republic's existence, the Kurds have been subjected to forty-nine years of war, violence, and siege, I still believe that war and violence are not our inevitable fate. We reject that fate. I am convinced that Kurds and Turks can live together peacefully within the borders of the same state and within the framework of democracy and respect for each other's rights, identity, and culture.

In truth, it does not seem to me to be so difficult to put an end to this war that darkens our future a little more each day and to create a just and lasting peace. For that, we must give up the policies, formulated more than eithty years ago, of the negation, destruction, and assimilation of the Kurds. We must take account of the sociological reality of Turkey and acknowledge that the Kurds, like all peoples, have democratic, cultural, and national rights that must be protected by legal and constitutional guarantees.

Spain, after the end of Franco's dictatorship, succeeded in establishing peace and stability by recognizing Basque and Catalan identity and culture and by giving the Basques and Catalanians ta large measure of autonomy.

I am fighting to see a new, modern, democratic Turkey that is free of militarism, official nationalist ideology, and the iron rule of political dinosaurs carry out the same kind of change, to see her acknowledge her cultural diversity not as weakness or threat, but as opportunity and resource. It is because of this struggle that my parliamentary colleagues and I have been behind bars for eithteen months.

The impact that our struggle has had in Germany, with its varied, complex links with Turkey and the Turkish peoples, and the interest that democratic, peace-loving Germans have shown us, has been a great moral support and source of pride to us.

I am aware that the prize your Association has awarded me is really being given, through me, to all Kurdish women, and through the women, to all Kurds who fight for peace, freedom, and democracy, and I thank you for it.

I would like to assure your Association and the participants in this ceremony that from now on I will be at your side in your work toward peace, and I wish you great success in your struggle.

Leyla Zana
Ankara Central Prison

Letter to Gro Harlem Brundtland
Prime Minister, Oslo, Norway

20 September 1995

Dear Prime Minister:

At this time, when the World Conference on Women is taking place, I feel impelled to write to you, the only woman Prime Minister in Western Europe, to ask for your help.

As you know, the Ankara State Security Court has sentenced me to fifteen years in prison for my political opinions and activities, and I have been in detention for the last eigtheen months in the Ankara Central Prison. As we cannot guess the results of my appeals to the Turkish Court of Appeals and the European Court of Human Rights, I do not know how much longer I will be held here, away from my children and all those dear to me.

However, apart from my own fate, what truly distresses me and drives me to write you this letter is the tragedy the Kurdish people are living in Turkey. Their situation is going from bad to worse: it is a terrible human tragedy with no pictures, no witnesses, lived in silence and indifference.

As the lone Kurdish woman parliamentarian in a Turkish Parliament of 450 members, I tried, despite threats, assassination attempts, and other methods of intimidation, to alert public opinion, in Turkey and the rest of the world, to my people's suffering, to bear witness and to struggle to end these sufferings, to put an end to war and violence, and to find a solution to our problems in the framework of democracy and through dialogue. The partisans of war who run our country fear that our testimony and our calls for peace and brotherhood might influence public opinion. That is why they have sentenced us to such long prison terms.

At the time of our arrest, the number of Kurdish villages forcibly evacuated and burned down was 847. One year later, according to official figures, the number of villages destroyed and burned down had risen to 2,665. By now, as I write this letter, about 3,500 villages will have been wiped off the map. In our mountains, millions of hectares of forest have been burned down, emptied of all human presence, so that no animals, domesticated or wild, can find shelter or survive. More than three million Kurds have been torn from their homes and their land, cast out onto the roads and abandoned in utter misery. Our people's millennial way of life, its traditional culture, and its economy have been destroyed. Over a large part of the fertile lands of Upper Mesopotamia, where humanity first developed agriculture, one can no longer farm or raise livestock. Our land, which only two or three years ago exported grain and meat to neighboring regions, now must import basic foodstuffs. I do not understand how those defenders of the environment, who mobilized world opinion to save three whales, can remain silent in face of the ecological disaster that is taking place in my country.

As a result of this exodus and the resulting unemployment and misery in the Kurdish regions, which until a few years ago enjoyed relatively decent living conditions, the per capita income had dropped to $204 in 1993 (to the level of Somalia or Bangladesh), against an average of $3,760 for Turkey as a whole. These two figures alone show, in the most striking manner, the gap created in Turkey between the Turkish and Kurdish regions and the dramatic dimensions of the injustice being inflicted on my people.

It is a fact that, just as clouds bring rain, so oppression and injustice generate hatred. The danger that this process will lead to a vast general conflagration, spreading to the whole of Turkey and the Turkish and Kurdish communities in Europe, should not be underestimated. The danger that a large portion of the Turkish and Kurdish masses, marginalized by the war, will slide into Islamic fundamentalism, either from sheer despair or as a reaction against the present nationalist and military regime, is steadily increasing.

It is obvious that this war which, in 1994 alone cost $12.5 billion dollars has become, for both the Turkish and Kurdish peoples, an economic, political, and moral disaster. If Turkey, despite all its attempts during the last seventy-two years, has been unable to resolve the Kurdish question by force of arms, it will not be able to stifle the claims to an identity and the democratic aspirations of its fifteen million Kurds by war and massacre. By the same token, it is impossible for the Kurds to win anything by violence and force of arms.

That is why it is imperative to stop this fratricidal bloodshed and silence the guns. It is time for the guns to fall silent and for the people to speak to one another and solve their problems through dialogue and compromise. However, it will require powerful outside support, respectable and without ulterior motives, to overcome the thick psychological wall erected between the two communities by long years of war and bloodshed and to initiate the process of dialogue.

In this respect, you and your country possess internationally recognized sensitivity and experience. I appeal to you as a mother, whose heart bleeds at the death of every young Turk or Kurd, as a person who believes that Kurds and Turks could live in Turkey in a democratic context, in friendship and equality, and who has devoted nearly half of her thirty-four years of life to the struggle for peace and human rights. I beg you to act so that your government pays greater attention to the Kurdish tragedy. We ask Norway, with its solid tradition of democracy and humanism, to act together with other countries, at least with the other Scandinavian countries, to bring this question before the United Nations, the Conference on Security and Cooperation in Europe [CSCE], and the Council of Europe so as to open up a peace initiative at the state level.

We have learned that a Kurdish-Turkish seminar on human rights took place in Oslo with the support of your government. We consider this a positive and useful start, and we are grateful and thank you for it. But the scale of the Kurdish tragedy requires an urgent and broad peace initiative at the government level. For forty-nine of the Turkish Republic's seventy-two-year existence, the Kurdish people have been subjected to wars, states of siege, violence, and persecution. Don't these people have the right to live like other peoples—in peace and tranquillity, devoting their energy to education and development and handing down their cultural heritage to their children? My people demand peace; they demand democracy; they want to live. One can say that, despite the warlike declarations of their leaders and the media, and despite all the brainwashing, the campaigns to discredit and silence the supporters of peace and brotherhood, the Turkish people, too, are tired of the war and favor a just solution to the Kurdish question within the existing borders. One of the most striking recent signs of this aspiration is the fact that Mrs. Tomris Ozden, widow of a colonel killed a few weeks earlier, following on her calls to stop fratricidal bloodshed and end the war, received a very high vote at the Congress of the Republican People's Party [CHP]. She was elected to its leadership, even though the CHP is a member of the government coalition and thus bears a share of responsibility for the war. Moreover, a large number of Turkish intellectuals and ordinary citizens publicly expressed their support for her. The intellectual dwarfs who brand all opponents of the war as "terrorists" and who have described the eminently respectable women presidents of three important European Parliament Groups as "prostitutes" because they dared concern themselves with the questions of human rights and democracy in Turkey, are now busy attacking this peace-loving, Turkish woman and orchestrating a media campaign to discredit her.

But our two peoples no longer believe what the famous writer Yasar Kemal (who is also facing prosecution) has called "the campaign of lies." That is why I believe that it is possible to launch a vast peace movement, with both Turkish and Kurdish women. In this struggle for peace and democracy we nonsectarian, peace-loving, and democratic women need the support of all women, of all who support democracy, peace, and religious tolerance. We must act together to stop Turkey from becoming another Bosnia, another Iran, another Algeria.

I am convinced that, both as a woman and as prime minister, you will not fail to support our call for peace and our struggle.

In this belief and in the hope that, together, we will succeed in making a better, more peaceful world for our children, please accept my sincerest greetings.

Yours respectfully,

Leyla Zana
Ankara Central Prison

Message to the European Parliament on Being Awarded the Sakharov Prize for Freedom of Thought

12 January 1996

Members of Parliament, dear colleagues:

It is a privilege and immense joy for me to be honored by the European Parliament with the Sakharov Prize. Of course, I would have loved to be with you today, to express my gratitude for this high honor personally, and to thank you warmly for your consistent efforts, over nearly two years, to obtain my liberation and that of my colleagues.

The implacable political realities of Turkey unfortunately prevent me from coming to Strasbourg. But the jailers who lock my body up behind the thick walls of an Ankara prison do not have the power to prevent my spirit from traveling freely. Therefore, in my thoughts, I will spend the day of 17 January with you.

I am particularly moved by being awarded the Sakharov Prize for a number of reasons. In the first instance, because it bears the name of one of the most important moral leaders of the century who is held in great respect by the Kurdish people. This man, imbued with a sense of justice and truth and long considered a defender of so-called lost or hopeless causes, was among the first to speak out and denounce the persecution of the Kurds by Saddam Hussein's dictatorship and to demand an end to the Soviet sale of arms to Baghdad. Several times over the years, he alerted public opinion to the fate of the Kurds deported and gassed in Iraq and massacred and displaced in Iran and Turkey. In Paris in October 1989, a few months before his death, he made a solemn public appeal in which, among other things, he said: "The tragic

---

Established in 1986, this prize is awarded for work in the defense of human rights and respect for international law, among other areas.

struggle of the Kurdish people, which has been going on for so long, is based on the principle of the right of a people to self-determination, and that is why it is just. I call on the governments, organizations, and citizens of every country, and on international organizations, in their dealings with the countries where the Kurds live, to take account of the true policies that the leaders of those countries are implementing towards the Kurds."

Denouncing injustice surely does not abolish it, nor does it heal the victims' wounds. But speaking out about their rights lends considerable moral support to the peoples who suffer in silence. No government heeded André Sakharov's call. But this great man nonetheless occupies a special place in the hearts and memories of the Kurds, alongside the American President Woodrow Wilson, who, from 1920 on, demanded the right to their own country for the Kurds, and the Swedish Prime Minister Olaf Palme and French President François Mitterrand, who demanded many times over that the rights of the Kurdish people be respected.

Defending the rights of the most humble, the pariahs of the international community like the Kurds or Tibetans, who have nothing to offer economically or politically, surely reflects true greatness of spirit. I respectfully salute those great men, with a very special thought for François Mitterrand, who has just passed away, and who showed interest in and friendship for my people, as well as for me personally.

The Sakharov Prize moves me also because of those who received it before me. Finding myself, thanks to your vote, in the spiritual family of Alexander Dubcek and Nelson Mandela awes and intimidates me. Fortunately, the Mothers of the Plaza del Mayo, Taslima Nasrin and Aung San Suu Kyi, keep me company and reassure me with their feminine presence and a form of struggle with which I can more easily identify. And I fully share the struggle of Serge Kovaliev, who was also proposed for this year's prize. In different contexts and by different means, we have both defended peoples who are the victims of savage military repression and a certain conception of human rights. Let me extend my greetings to Mr. Kovaliev, not a rival but a companion in struggle, a worthy heir of André Sakharov, who would have made an excellent recipient of your prize this year.

I think that you took a risk in deciding to award the prize to me, knowing full well that you were going to ratify the Customs Union Treaty with Turkey a few weeks later—the risk of giving the world a mixed message. Is it possible to satisfy both the most repressive regime in Europe and some of its victims? By awarding the Sakharov Prize to a Kurdish political prisoner, you express your commitment to the defense of human rights and democratic freedoms. Through me you demonstrate your sympathy for the suffering Kurdish people, particularly the courageous Kurdish women, who resist and do not submit to brute force and oppression, and you express the wish for a humane, political settlement of the Kurdish problem. For that is the essence of the cause that my colleagues and I are defending. That is why we were convicted, and that is why we are in prison.

At the same time, although the Turkish government has not met your demands for fundamental democratic reform, you have ratified the Customs Union Treaty. We are hoping that your gesture will help the democratic forces, strengthen the democracy movement, and block the advance of the Islamic fundamentalists. In the East, people tend to rely on God's wisdom. Do you tend to rely on the good will and wisdom of the Turkish government?

You know that this government, in four years, has evacuated and wiped off the map more than three thousand of our villages, set fire to our mountains and forests, drove three million Kurds into exile, wandering, and misery, and ordered the murders of 105 political leaders of the legal pro-Kurdish parties HEP [People's Labor Party], DEP [Democracy Party], and HADEP [People's Democracy Party], including one member of Parliament, as well as more than 3,000 pacifist Kurdish intellectuals. That is why we are wounded to the quick. Put yourself in the place of the Kurds for a moment. What would you have thought?

In 1995, the situation is hardly any better. In one year nearly 6,000 citizens were judged for crimes of opinion, 1,200 cases of serious torture were recorded, and 184 people disappeared while in custody. And it goes on. During the past week alone, 79 people appeared before the Istanbul Security Court for crimes of opinion; a Turkish journalist, Metin Göktepe, died in police custody; and a highly respected former Kurdish member of Parliament, Abdülmelik Firat, was arrested.

In spite of this somber picture, I hope, for everyone's sake, that your gamble proves to be correct. If not, our people's faith in the principles and values of European democracy will be shaken. And lack of faith in democracy could open the way to dangerous excesses and ventures. Please be aware that by accepting the Sakharov Prize in this context, I also am taking a risk. The risk is that public opinion may see my action as a consolation prize and may not understand why I would participate in a game like this. But I do not avoid risk or danger. I accept this award without hesitation and with my head held high in order to continue to develop our dialogue and to express my gratitude for everything that you have done for us so far. There is no other reasonable choice but dialogue. In many ways Turkey is part of Europe. Nearly three million Turks and Kurds live and work in the nations of the European Union. The Kurdish question is now also a European question. Europe must, sooner or later, find a solution to the Kurdish question, not only for the stability of its ally Turkey, but also to ensure order and internal peace in the countries of the Union. A solution will be found only through dialogue, multilateral dialogue. A dialogue between Kurds and Turks, between Kurds and Europeans, between Europeans and Turks. We Kurds must make the effort to convince our Turkish neighbors, who have undergone more than seventy years of nationalist brainwashing, of the justice of our cause. A few months ago, François Mitterrand declared before this very Parliament: "Nationalism is war." This is highly pertinent observation, for one people's nationalism creates and exacerbates that of others. And people end up killing each other, as in my country. It is time to put a stop to this killing.

The Europeans probably do not know the Kurds except through the Turkish government's biased propaganda. We, the Kurds, must convince the European democrats that not all Kurds are terrorists, and that it is neither terrorism nor separatism to fight to defend one's language and culture. Just as no one could, in the name of European unity, demand that the smaller nations give up their languages and cultures and submit to the supremacy of German, English, or French, no one has the right, in the name of Turkish unity, to require the fifteen to twenty million Kurds of Turkey to give up their language and culture and become Turks. For seventy-two years now Turkey has tried, by means of a policy of war, terror, deportation, massacre, and prohibition, to make the Kurdish people disappear from the face of the earth as a distinct people, with a language, culture, and identity of their own.

Dear fellow Parliamentarians, I respectfully ask you, what would you have done if you were Kurds in Turkey?

Some may accept assimilation. It is certainly their right, and I respect that right. But there must also be acknowledgment of the rights of millions of other citizens who want to preserve the legacy of their ancestors; to defend their millennial language, history, and culture, and hand them down to their children; to have their own schools, radio, and television; and to live in freedom on their own land. Who, in the name of what cause and by what right, can deprive them of these fundamental human rights? There is no question of creating another state or of modifying existing borders. This is a fundamental question of humanity and respect for others.

I believe that my people's cause is just. And I know that in our peaceful, democratic struggle our main weapon, here and abroad, is persuasion. It is essential to develop a dialogue with you. I think that the dialogue begun nearly two years ago has been mutually enriching. Thanks to your delegations' visits, we have a better understanding of your approach to problems and your conception of democracy and freedom.

And I imagine that for your part, you now know Turkey, its political system, its leaders, and its justice much better. But I deeply regret that none of your delegations have ever gone to the country's Kurdish provinces. Just as the Palestinian problem cannot truly be understood without visiting the Gaza Strip, the extent and gravity of the Kurdish problem in Turkey cannot be grasped without a trip to Kurdistan. I urge you to go there. Go and see for yourselves what has become of that fertile land of Upper Mesopotamia, blessed by God! Go and see the thousands of our villages evacuated and destroyed, our mountains and forests set on fire, our traditional rural economy dismantled, all in the name of the fight against terrorism. In fact, however, the scorched-earth policy itself, the terrible, massive repression (which a Turkish minister, Mr. Köylüoglu, has called "state terrorism") fuels the revolt in a well-known spiral. Go and see the misery of millions of displaced Kurds, chased from their homes! Ask yourselves about the exorbitant economic, human, social, and political costs of the Kurdish conflict. Ask yourselves about the link between this conflict and the army's grip on the political life of the country, on the link between this conflict and the development of Islamic fundamentalism among the people, marginalized by the war and disillusioned with traditional Turkish parties. You will then understand better why a man as ideologically and socially removed from us as Halis Komilli, president of the association of Turkish employers, considered the Kurdish problem the number one political problem in the country, and the key to any democratization. Even a conservative politician like the leader of the Motherland Party now declares that there can be no true democratization without a settlement of the Kurdish problem in Turkey.

The great majority of the Turkish people also want peace and a political settlement of the Kurdish problem. But the Turkish army and the political parties it controls are not even willing to accept the existence of a Kurdish problem, and this intransigent policy has brought our country to its current predicament.

I know that Western governments consider Turkey an important ally because of its geographic position. However, Turkey is not merely geography or a market. What is the strategic value of a country that does not enjoy peace or internal stability? Once again, the key to stability and to a lasting peace is the Kurdish problem, because it is the Kurds who border on Iran, Iraq, and Syria.

Dear colleagues:
The message that I want to send you from my prison is this: My people fervently desire peace, the recognition of their dignity and identity, and democracy. In the seventy-two years of the Turkish Republic's history, my people have endured forty-nine years of martial law and emergency rule,[1] persecution, deporta-

tion and humiliation. My people are tired of war and violence. The Kurdish people want to see the page of war and oppression turned. We feel no rancor. My family and I have suffered great hardship and persecution, but I do not feel hatred for anyone. My only passion is justice. The death of an innocent Turk in this absurd war distresses me as much as that of a Kurd. I am ready to forgive. Nor are my people inspired by hatred; they are not hostile to the Turks. They want to turn over this black page in the history of Kurdish-Turkish relations definitively and are prepared to pardon their oppressors. Although, of course, to pardon does not mean to forget.

We are waiting for a humanistic president to arise from among the Turks, for him to go to Diyarbakir, to go down on his knees and ask forgiveness of the Kurdish people for the suffering and humiliation inflicted on them during the last seventy-two years, to give us heart. Then we will be able to open a new page of our history together.

Maybe I am dreaming. But dreams of yesterday have become reality. After so many years of war and killing, the French, Germans, English and other European peoples succeeded in making peace with one another and are today building the European Union together, and their representatives sit in your Parliament. The time has also come for reconciliation between Kurds and Turks.

I think that today it is possible to find a political solution to the Kurdish problem within the framework of democracy and within the context of existing borders. A three-point plan could, with your help and help from the European Union and the United States, begin the peace process:

1. A bilateral cease-fire for an indeterminate period;
2. A general amnesty of all political prisoners;
3. Legislative reform to permit freedom of activity of all Kurdish political parties that reject violence and respect the country's territorial integrity.

The Kurdish people would then be able freely to elect their representatives, who would be mandated to defend their goals. It would be up to those elected officials to negotiate with the government on the political reforms necessary to guarantee Kurdish cultural and linguistic rights and to rebuild and develop Kurdistan.

You could help by creating a special Parliamentary Committee for information and mediation, which would bring together the diverse strands of the indispensable dialogue. Once the Kurdish conflict is settled, no one will join in armed struggle and terrorism, Turkey will not have to waste its resources and energy in colossal military expenditures, and the army will have no pretext for maintaining its grip on the country. There will be no serious reason for Islamic fundamentalism to gain ground. We will then see Turkey truly rooted in democratic Europe.

Without the settlement of the Kurdish problem, without vast state reform and the establishment of a truly democratic system, Turkey will always be the sick man of Europe, and Europe will become sicker and sicker because of Turkey. Today, Turkey is seriously ill. It cannot be treated by pain killers or simple massage. For its survival, it needs serious treatment. And the Kurdish and Turkish democrats are working for this.

Beyond the borders and divisions of language, religion, and culture, we share certain universal values of freedom and human rights. It is in the name of these values that you have honored me with the Sakharov Prize, and it is in the name of these same values that I ask for your help to put an end to the tragedy of my people and to build a democratic, pluralistic, European Turkey, respectful of its own cultural diversity.

With this hope, I again express my thanks, and cordially greet each one of you.

Leyla Zana
Ankara Central Prison

1. Under emergency rule, Constitutional law is suspended and the Kurdish provinces are governed directly by a governor or army commander.

On the Occasion of *Nevruz*

March 1998

My Dear Friends,

The duty of any party or political organization is periodically to inform and educate its cadres and sympathizers in order to prepare them for the future.

To this effect, the party must stress internal education, seminars, meetings, and similar activities, and then to spread this information to the general public through monthly bulletins.

The bulletin is a very important source of information about the policies, ideas, and perspectives of the party's leadership. It is extremely difficult for a people like ours, (exploited, treated as if they didn't exist, and facing deportation and destruction) to create the institutions for political action. Nevertheless, the important thing is to overcome these difficulties. Thus, we must state frankly that we have not sufficiently improved ourselves since the time of the HEP[1] in this respect. The party's central authority is nor recognized, and discipline is not accepted. We present ourselves as an organized movement, but we do not act in an organized manner. We could go on listing the shortcomings.

We must not forget that the legal struggle has been carried out to this level at the cost of intense effort and great sacrifice. HADEP (People's Democracy Party), heir to the HEP (People's Labor Party) and the DEP (Democracy Party) has dozens of martyrs and as many prisoners. Vedat Aydin, Mehmet Sincar, and Muhsin Melik[2] are only some names among many others. We must not forget that the democratic gains we are trying to preserve were attained through the martyrdom of these comrades.

On 17 September, the very day that the European Parliament, in another resolution, called for the immediate release of Mrs. Leyla Zana, the Ankara State Security Court sentenced the former M.P. to an additional two years jail for this message, which appeared in the HADEP internal bulletin on the occasion of *Nevruz*, the Kurdish New Year. (Courtesy of CILDEKT—International Committee for the Liberation of Kurdish Parliamentarians Imprisoned in Turkey— Update on the State of Affairs in Turkey, No. 112, October 7, 1998.)

That is why we must understand that we have no right to act against the will of the people or to squander the values created. Similarly, we must understand that precisely what differentiates us from the Establishment Parties is that we base ourselves on the people's own strength, and we can act because of the support and courage we can draw from the people.

As long as we are sincere in our intentions and as long as our shortcomings and even our faults do not harm the struggle for democracy and freedom, they will be forgiven by the people.

We must know that our people will not accept approaches based on egotism, ulterior motives, career goals, and personal self-interest. At a time when the war is becoming more and more intense and we are passing through a difficult period, we must set aside personal interests and selfishness and remain united.

Affectionately,

Leyla Zana,
Member of Parliament, in prison

1. HEP is the People's Labor Party, on whose list Leyla Zana and about twenty of her colleagues were elected in November 1991. The HEP was later banned by the Turkish Constitutional Court.
2. These HEP leaders were assassinated by death squads. Mehmet Sincar was M.P. for Mardin at the time of his assassination.

Appendix-A

Amnesty International—Report—EUR 44/85/97 December 1997

Turkey—The Colours of Their Clothes: Parliamentary Deputies Serve 15 Years' Imprisonment for Expressions of Kurdish Political Identity

"That the defendant Lelya Zana on 18 October 1991 did wear clothes and accessories in yellow, green, red while addressing the people of Cizre on 18 October 1991"

> —Part of the grounds cited in convicting Leyla Zana
> (Verdict of Ankara State Security Court No 1, page 555)

On 8 December 1994, after proceedings which fell deplorably short of international standards governing fair trials, four deputies of the Turkish parliament, Leyla Zana, Hatip Dicle, Selim Sadak and Orhan Dogan, were convicted at Ankara State Security Court of membership in an illegal armed organization, the Kurdish Workers' Party [PKK],[1] under Article 168/1 of the Turkish Penal Code. The four members of Parliament were each sentenced to fifteen years' imprisonment.

On 30 November 1995 the United Nations [UN] Working Group on Arbitrary Detention ruled the imprisonment of the four to be arbitrary, in contravention of Articles 10 and 11 of the Universal Declaration of Human Rights. The Working Group requested the Turkish Government "to take the necessary steps to remedy the situation,"[2] which it has failed to do. Leyla Zana, Hatip Dicle, Selim Sadak and Orhan Dogan continue to serve their terms of imprisonment in Ankara Central Closed Prison.

Proceedings against the four deputies were prompted by an incident at their inauguration as members of Parliament, when Leyla Zana and Hatip Dicle made statements in Kurdish and wore traditional Kurdish colours. Amnesty International considers that the deputies are prisoners of conscience, imprisoned for the expression of their peaceful beliefs, and is appealing for their immediate and unconditional release.

Expression of Kurdish Identity in Parliament Leads to Trial and Imprisonment

Leyla Zana, Hatip Dicle, Selim Sadak and Orhan Dogan were elected in October 1991 to serve in Parliament as representatives of the Social Democrat Populist Party [SHP]. While in office they resigned from SHP, transferring their allegiance and their parliamentary seats first to the People's Labour Party [HEP] and later, after HEP was closed down by the authorities in 1993 for "separatism," to the newly-formed Democracy Party [DEP]. DEP was a party of the left which challenged the policies of the Turkish state towards the Kurds and which, in Leyla Zana's words, sought to bring about "reconciliation between Kurds and Turks." The four deputies are themselves members of Turkey's large Kurdish minority.[3] DEP was closed down by the Turkish Constitutional Court on 16 June 1994 on the grounds of its "separatist" activities and the deputies then lost their parliamentary seats (see appendix [to this article] for the history of the Kurdish parliamentary parties and the intense political repression they have experienced).

At their inauguration as members of Parliament in 1991, Leyla Zana and Hatip Dicle made brief statements in Kurdish, and Leyla Zana wore the traditional Kurdish colours of red, yellow and green in her headband.[4] Orhan Dogan and Hatip Dicle wore handkerchiefs in their breast pockets in the same colours. After taking the oath of loyalty in Turkish as required, Leyla Zana added in Kurdish: "I have completed this formality under duress. I shall struggle so that the Kurdish and Turkish peoples may live peacefully together in a democratic framework."[5] These actions provoked pandemonium in the parliamentary chamber. There were cries of "separatist!," "traitor!," "arrest her!" and even "hang her!," and legal proceedings were immediately initiated. Although the deputies were initially protected from prosecution by their parliamentary immunity, in February 1994 Prime Minister Tansu Çiller and the Chief of General Staff began moves which eventually brought about the deputies' trial and conviction.[6]

On 22 February 1994 Tansu Çiller was reported as saying: "The time has come to deal with this issue of the PKK sheltering under the roof of Parliament." When deputies from her party shouted that Hatip Dicle, the then president of DEP, was a traitor, Tansu Çiller responded, "That is correct. He is exactly that!"[7] On the same day the newspaper *Cumhuriyet* (Republic) quoted General Güres, then Chief of General Staff, as saying of the DEP deputies: "If these are not traitors, then who is?"

On 2 March, the deputies' parliamentary immunity was lifted and the countdown for their prosecution on charges of treason began. There were irregularities about the lifting of the deputies' parliamentary immunity. A publication by the Inter-Parliamentary Union [IPU][8] quoted the President of the Turkish parliament's view that the public statement of Prime Minister Çiller made at the opening of one of her party's group meetings ("Our mission is to lift the shadow of the PKK hovering over Parliament") provided grounds for annulling the Parliament's decision to lift immunity, since Article 85, paragraph 5, of the Turkish Constitution prohibits such discussions within party groups.

Leyla Zana, Hatip Dicle and Orhan Dogan were detained between 2 and 4 March and held in incommunicado detention for

---

Leyla Zana

Leyla Zana was born in the village of Bahçe, Diyarbakir province in 1961. She married at the age of fifteen and is mother of two children, Ronay and Ruken.

Her husband, Mehdi Zana, former mayor of Diyarbakir, was severely tortured and imprisoned following the 12 September 1980 military coup. Leyla Zana visited him regularly in prison until his release in 1991. This experience drew her into politics and human rights activism. She founded a movement of prisoners' families and worked for the Diyarbakir branch of the Human Rights Association [HRA]. In October 1991 she was elected as a member of Parliament for Diyarbakir.

Arrested in July 1988, she was herself severely tortured. She still bears the physical and psychological scars of these abuses and her health is fragile. Mehdi Zana is now a refugee in Sweden and their two children live in France.

between twelve and fourteen days before being committed to prison. Selim Sadak was detained on 1 July. Extended incommunicado police detention [detention unsupervised by a judge] constitutes a breach of Article 5 of the European Convention for the Protection of Human Rights and Fundamental Freedoms. On 26 November 1997 the European Court of Human Rights ruled that the deputies' incommunicado detention was unlawful and breached Turkey's commitments under the Convention. Turkey was ordered to pay a total of nearly US$50,000 in compensation to the deputies. (A second petition lodged by the deputies in January 1996 against their conviction is still under consideration by the European Commission on Human Rights.)

Unfair Trial

"The action being brought against my Kurdish parliamentary colleagues and myself represents a first in Turkish political history. It is in fact the first time that, under a supposedly civilian government, elected representatives of the people have been arbitrarily jailed and brought to trial for their opinions and threatened with death sentences. This trial really has no legal basis. It is entirely political."

— Leyla Zana

As prisoners of conscience, the four deputies should never have been brought to trial. Nevertheless, the first hearing opened at Ankara State Security Court on 3 August 1994. The four deputies[9] were initially charged with "treason," for which the prosecutor demanded the death penalty, but during the course of the trial this was reduced to the lesser charge of membership of an illegal armed organization. The initial hearings were observed by an Amnesty International delegate.

In the indictment the Ankara State Security Court prosecutor quoted extensively from the deputies' public speeches and writings in which they speak of the Kurdish minority as a group with a distinct identity. These speeches and writings—which make no advocacy of violence, and include such activities as signing a petition to the Organization for Security and Co-operation in Europe [OSCE] and preparing a declaration to the United Nations—were presented as evidence of membership of the PKK.

The testimony which supposedly connected the four deputies to the PKK was highly suspect. The most incriminating statements were obtained from people who themselves faced prosecution, but who had turned state's evidence in return for a lighter punishment, or from people who later retracted their statements claiming that these had been extracted under torture. Abdulvahap Kandemir, for example, had given a statement in police custody that Orhan Dogan had sheltered him in his parliamentary lodging in July 1993 in the full knowledge that he was a member of the PKK. Orhan Dogan was convicted on the basis of this statement. Abdulvahap Kandemir reportedly retracted this statement, stating that it had been extracted under torture while he was being held in incommunicado detention. Amnesty International is not aware that any efforts were made by the Turkish authorities to investigate Abdulvahap Kandemir's allegation of torture, or to ensure that such a statement taken under torture was not used in court, as they are bound to do under the UN Convention against Torture.

Orhan Dogan

Orhan Dogan was born in 1955 in the Derik district of Mardin province. He is a lawyer by profession—a graduate of Ankara University Law Faculty—but for a time was an official in Ankara's Primary School Education Directorate. After the 1980 military coup he resigned as a state employee and started working as a lawyer in the district of Cizre, Sirnak province.

Orhan Dogan devoted a great deal of time working for the Sirnak branch of the HRA. Bomb attacks against his home and workplace in 1989, 1990 and 1991 caused severe damage. In the October 1991 general elections he was elected as a member of parliament for Sirnak.

His wife and four of his five children, aged between nine and sixteen, now live in Ankara. A fifth daughter is studying at university in France.

Many statements were collected over the months after the deputies were detained—conveying the strong impression that the prosecution had attempted to create a body of evidence to support the thin charges on which the deputies were originally arrested. Typical of such statements was that of Sedat Bucak—the most damning evidence presented by the prosecution.

Sedat Bucak is a member of Parliament and leader of a powerful Kurdish clan in the Siverek region of southeast Turkey[10] who testified to the Ankara State Prosecutor that Leyla Zana tried repeatedly to persuade him to collude with the PKK by allowing them to fight on his land. The indictment contains what is purported to be a transcript of a tape of such a conversation, although the defence was never given a copy of the tape. In fact the three-page transcript consists mainly of a record of a conversation between Sedat Bucak and another man. Leyla Zana herself speaks only forty-two unincriminating words, but Sedat Bucak presented this as part of a series of conversations amounting to conspiracy, and the State Security Court accepted his testimony.

However, Sedat Bucak was thoroughly discredited as a witness when, on 3 November 1996, his car crashed near the town of Susurluk in northwestern Turkey. He was the only survivor, but weapons apparently intended for use in assassinations—automatic firearms with silencers—were found in the car, and one of his fellow travellers was a man who, in spite of the fact that he was wanted by police as a leader of a right-wing death squad and drug-smuggler, had been given credentials by the Interior Ministry under an assumed name. There were other grave irregularities in the trial. Most importantly, the court did not give the defence an opportunity to test the prosecution evidence. For example, the court refused to check the alibis of those deputies accused by so-called "confessors" (former PKK members who had turned state's evidence in return for a reduction in sentence) of having visited the PKK's Zeli camp near the Iranian border. Moreover, the testimony of the "confessors" was contradictory—some saying that the deputies had visited the camp, others saying that although they were expected, they had never arrived. Copies of tapes used in evidence against the deputies were never supplied to the defence. Nor did the court permit the defence to call as witnesses those who had given testimony used by the prosecution and examine them. On 24 November 1994 a request by the defence lawyer for witnesses to be called was refused by the Court. As a result, the deputies announced they would no longer present a defence because they did not believe the Court was impartial.

On 8 December 1994 all four were convicted by Ankara State Security Court of membership in the PKK under Article 168/1 of the Turkish Penal Code and sentenced to fifteen years' imprisonment. The sentences were confirmed by the Court of Appeal on 26 October 1995.

Prisoners of Conscience

Leyla Zana, Hatip Dicle, Orhan Dogan and Selim Sadak were never accused of any acts of violence or of advocacy of violence. Indeed most of the statements for which they were convicted contained strong pleas for a peaceful solution to the conflict in southeast Turkey and an end to the bloodshed. The verdict relied heavily on the deputies' public speeches and writings quoted in the indictment—in which the deputies repeatedly assert the Kurdish minority to be a group with a distinct identity but do not advocate violence—as evidence of their membership in the PKK. The acts condemned by the judgment as being evidence of membership in the PKK include: a press statement in connection with

---

Selim Sadak

Selim Sadak was born in 1954 in a village in Idil district, Sirnak province. He graduated from the mathematics department of Diyarbakir's Education Institute.

Selim Sadak was actively involved in local politics for many years and stood as mayor of Idil on two occasions. He joined the SHP in 1987 and in the October 1991 general election he was elected as an SHP member of Parliament for Sirnak, later transferring his seat to HEP and then to DEP.

Selim Sadak is married and has 10 children, aged between six and twenty-one. His eldest son is a refugee in Germany. His wife and remaining children live in Ankara.

the swearing of the parliamentary oath; the "wearing of yellow, green and red accessories" while swearing the oath; a public statement to the United Nations on 2 April 1992 calling for investigation of the killing of civilians during disturbances at the time of Nevruz, the Kurdish New Year, of 21 March 1992; and a petition of 20 November 1991 to the Conference on Security and Co-operation in Europe (now the Organization for Security and Co-operation in Europe—OSCE) calling for that organization to appoint a human rights monitoring body to Turkey.

After close examination of the indictment and verdict Amnesty International has concluded that none of the evidence confirms the allegation of membership in the PKK. DEP parliamentarians did have contacts with the PKK, but these contacts were not only unsurprising, given the fact that they had been elected principally to bring an end to the decade of bloodshed occasioned by the conflict between the PKK and the Turkish State, but were also sanctioned by the State. In early 1993 some of the DEP deputies had met the then President Turgut Özal, who agreed that they should mediate in the conflict, and gave his blessing to a mission to Damascus, Syria, to meet Abdullah Öcalan, the leader of the PKK. During this mission, which resulted in an extension of a cease-fire, they were welcomed by an official from the Turkish embassy in Syria.

The political establishment of Turkey views discussion of minority rights, education in Kurdish or regional autonomy as close to treachery. Even completely non-violent advocacy of separatism is punishable by up to three years' imprisonment under Article 8 of the Antiterror Law. The State, not yet ready to enter into a debate about the status of its ethnic minorities, has continued to shut down parties and imprison politicians who insist on raising such questions and has also resorted to illegal methods to suppress political opposition. More than 160 members of DEP and its predecessor and successor parties have been killed or "disappeared" since 1991.

In a letter smuggled out of prison, extracts of which were published in European newspapers in September 1994, Leyla Zana made clear the peaceful character of her beliefs and hopes for the future of Turkish society: "I have appealed for peace and dialogue. My crime has been to use a Kurdish phrase for the friendship of Kurds and Turks and their coexistence during my oath of loyalty in Parliament. Even the colour of my clothes are supposed to make me a 'separatist.' "

She continues: "In speaking of the existence of the Kurdish people, of its country Kurdistan, in peaceably calling for the recognition of the Kurdish culture and identity in a democratic framework and within existing frontiers, I am supposed to have defended the same objectives as the PKK and therefore to be 'objectively a member of the political wing of that party,' which is engaged in an armed struggle; whereas all our action was aimed at silencing the guns and of seeking a peaceful solution to the Kurdish problem."[11]

Turkey is a signatory to the European Convention for the Protection of Human Rights and Fundamental Freedoms. Article 10 of that Convention safeguards the right to freedom of expression.

Hatip Dicle

Hatip Dicle was born in Diyarbakir in 1955. He graduated from Istanbul Technical University as a construction engineer. In 1979 he took up a position as President of the Chamber of Construction Engineers. Between 1982 and 1989 he worked for the State Highways Office as engineer on a number of road-building projects throughout Turkey. In 1984 Hatip Dicle was detained for two months in Mamak Military Prison in Ankara on suspicion of being "a member of an illegal organization."

In 1989 he returned to Diyarbakir, where he helped found a housing construction cooperative. In June 1990 he was elected as President of the HRA's Diyarbakir branch, and in October of the same year was elected to the HRA's national General Executive Committee. In the 1991 general election Hatip Dicle was elected as an SHP member of Parliament for Diyarbakir. He then served as HEP's deputy party leader and was subsequently elected as party leader of DEP.

His mother, father (retired) and sister live in the family home in Diyarbakir.

Interpretation of this article in an unrelated case at the European Court of Human Rights in 1976 emphasized the need for robust defence of expressions of opinion, even when they run counter to the prevailing official view:

"Freedom of expression constitutes one of the essential foundations of such [democratic] society, one of the basic conditions for its progress and for the development of every man. Subject to Article 10(2), it is applicable not only to 'information' or 'ideas' that are favourably received or regarded as inoffensive or as a matter of indifference, but also to those that offend, shock or disturb the State or any sector of the population. Such are the demands of that pluralism, tolerance and broadmindedness without which there is no 'democratic society.' "[12]

The Turkish Government continues to fail this test, persisting instead in stifling all discussion of the issue of ethnic minorities in Turkey, such as the debate DEP and its members of parliament were attempting to initiate.

Amnesty International believes not only that Leyla Zana, Hatip Dicle, Orhan Dogan and Selim Sadak were convicted after an unfair trial which should never have taken place at all, but that they are prisoners of conscience, imprisoned purely for the peaceful expression of their beliefs. Amnesty International calls for the immediate and unconditional release of the four deputies.

International Calls for Deputies' Release

A wave of international criticism followed the arrest and imprisonment of the four deputies and has continued. On 11 March 1994, the European Parliament passed a resolution calling for the release of the deputies and condemning "this attack on pluralist democracy" and upon "democratically elected MPs whose only crime is to have defended the interests of the Kurdish people in Turkey." A second European Parliament resolution calling for the deputies' release was issued on 5 October, followed by a third on 15 December when the Parliament condemned ". . . all aspects of the trial, the verdict handed down against the [members of Parliament] and the outlawing of their party."

On 12 April 1994 the Parliamentary Assembly of the Council of Europe passed a resolution calling on the Turkish authorities to withdraw the charges against the deputies, stating that their arrest was "of a criminal nature [and] a possible threat to the very essence of parliamentary democracy." On 30 November 1995 the UN Working Group on Arbitrary Detention ruled the deputies' imprisonment to be arbitrary.

In April 1996 the Inter-Parliamentary Union [IPU] passed a resolution in Istanbul calling for the deputies to be released pending proceedings before the European Commission on Human Rights. In July 1996 the OSCE's Parliamentary Assembly appealed for the release of all prisoners detained solely for non-violent expression of their views, including the four deputies. This was followed on 21 September by a further IPU resolution in Beijing which reiterated the hope that the deputies would be released pending the proceedings before the European Commission.

Successive Turkish governments have remained unmoved in the face of such high-level condemnations and appeals. Meanwhile Leyla Zana, Hatip Dicle, Orhan Dogan and Selim Sadak continue to be held at Ankara Central Closed Prison. The four are permitted to associate with each other during the day, but are only allowed to see their families once a week in "closed" meetings behind barred glass windows. Leyla Zana is not permitted to speak by telephone to her husband and two teenage children, all of whom live abroad.

While in prison Hatip Dicle has received further sentences for his writings. Leyla Zana was nominated for the Nobel Peace Prize in 1995, and in November of the same year the European Parliament awarded her the Sakharov Prize for the defence of human rights, awarded in previous years to, among others, Nelson Mandela and Aung San Suu Kyi. Her husband, Mehdi Zana, who was mayor of Diyarbakir when he was arrested in 1980 and imprisoned by the military junta for eleven years, received the prize on his wife's behalf in January 1996[13] and read out her acceptance statement:

"I think that a political solution could now be found to the Kurdish problem, working within existing frontiers and the democratic system. Maybe I am dreaming. Yet some of yesterday's dreams have become living realities. After long years of war and slaughter, the French, Germans, British and other European peoples have managed to make peace and today are together building the European Union. The time has likewise come for reconciliation between Kurds and Turks."

Unless the Turkish authorities take steps to remedy the situation, as they were instructed to do by the UN Working Group on Arbitrary Detention, the four deputies will remain in prison until at least 2005.[14] Amnesty International will continue to campaign on behalf of Leyla Zana and her fellow imprisoned members of Parliament, and to put pressure on the Turkish authorities until all four are unconditionally released.

Appendix

The trial, conviction and imprisonment of the four deputies was just one act in a drama of intense political repression in which they and other members of their party were faced with daily official harassment and the constant threat of being tortured, "disappeared" or killed.

Kurdish Political Parties under fire

The People's Labour Party [HEP] was founded in June 1990 by a group of deputies who resigned from the Social Democrat Populist Party [SHP]. HEP enjoyed extraordinary electoral success. In the 1991 general election a group of twenty-one deputies from HEP, including Leyla Zana, Hatip Dicle, Orhan Dogan and Selim Sadak, were elected while standing on the SHP ticket. In August 1993 HEP was closed down for "separatism" by the Constitutional Court, but it was succeeded by DEP, which was founded in May 1993.

Police, prosecutors and that sector of the media which supported the government policies in the southeast assumed that DEP was the "legal wing" of the PKK. But in fact DEP represented a broad front of Kurdish political views, doubtless including PKK sympathizers, but also others who had for years strongly and publicly opposed the PKK's violent methods. DEP was not the political wing of the PKK and no serious evidence was brought to the trial of Leyla Zana, Hatip Dicle, Orhan Dogan and Selim Sadak in support of this allegation. Yet DEP became a repository for the aspirations of many of the Kurdish population, thereby bringing it in direct conflict with the official doctrine of the Turkish State.

After DEP's closure—again for "separatism"—in June 1994, it was succeeded in turn by the People's Democracy Party [HADEP], which has so far survived as a legally authorized political party. HADEP opposes the use of political violence, but because its political goals to some extent resemble those of the PKK, the party is—like DEP—regarded in some quarters as the PKK's "political wing."

Harassment . . .

Because of their opposition to state policy towards the Kurdish minority, officials from all three parties [HEP, DEP, and HADEP] encountered official harassment on a routine basis. Local party headquarters, particularly in the southeast but also in Ankara and Istanbul, were frequently raided by police—raids notable for their brutality and wanton material destruction. Likely voters were intimidated. In the local elections of 27 March 1994 a number of communities reported that villagers had been threatened by gendarmes [soldiers] that they would be burned out of their homes if votes for DEP appeared in the ballot box for their district. Such intimidation was so widespread that DEP was forced to withdraw from these elections.

The case of Abdullah Kaya illustrates the extent of official suspicion with which any DEP member was regarded. Abdullah Kaya was SHP mayor of Kozluk, Batman province, who in 1992 was recognized by the Interior Ministry as an outstanding community politician and nominated for the King Baudouin Development Award, an annual prize awarded in Belgium to honour Europe's best local administrators. In September 1993 Abdullah Kaya transferred to DEP. On 9 February 1994 he was expelled from his post by the Interior Ministry. No explanation for his expulsion was ever given.[15]

Leyla Zana and her fellow deputies were subjected to a smear campaign in the media and in Parliament itself, where they were branded as members of the PKK. The press and the security forces collaborated on several occasions to produce completely groundless stories intended to demonize the DEP deputies. The newspaper *Meydan* [Open Space] published on 23 January 1992 a story entitled "Horrific confession" in which Emel Dogu, a young woman, presented as a PKK militant responsible for killing police officers, was said to have described how Leyla Zana and her husband Mehdi Zana allowed wounded PKK activists to be given medical treatment in their home in Diyarbakir. In a later statement, Emel Dogu described how she had been arrested and tortured by being stripped naked, sexually assaulted, beaten, suspended by the arms and subjected to electric shocks in incommunicado detention for twenty-four days before being brought to court where she was released on 28 January 1992. She publicly refuted the whole Meydan story, and it emerged that at the time at which they were supposed to have invited wanted militants into their home, Leyla Zana was in Istanbul and her husband was abroad.

. . . and Murder

Legal sanctions increasingly gave way to political killing as a means of silencing the dissent of Kurdish democrats. More than 160 officials and members of HEP, DEP and HADEP have been shot dead, "disappeared" or tortured to death in police custody since 1991.

Leyla Zana and her fellow DEP members of parliament were subjected to death threats throughout their incumbency as members of parliament. On 18 April 1992 Orhan Dogan was witness to a conversation at Tepe village, Diyarbakir province, in which a gendarmerie colonel, accompanied by a police chief, reportedly told Leyla Zana: "I am going to kill you, but first I am going to discredit you."[16] On 8 May 1992 Amnesty International issued an alert (See Urgent Action, AI Index: EUR 44/44/92) in connection with a death threat being circulated against the four deputies and twenty-four others. On 30 July 1992, Amnesty International issued another alert in response to what appeared to be an attempt to abduct and kill Leyla and Mehdi Zana in Istanbul. On 8 March 1993 Leyla Zana was nearly run over by a police armoured car which reportedly charged a public rally which she was addressing in Cizre, Sirnak province.

On 15 March 1993, the Turkish Embassy in Dublin wrote in complacent terms to an Irish member of Parliament who had raised concern about the safety of Leyla Zana, and in particular the threat which she reported having received from the gendarmerie colonel in April 1992:

"The death threat which Mrs. Zana allegedly received from the gendarmerie commander cannot be serious. I am amazed that you have attributed credence to these obviously manufactured allegations. The life and safety of Mrs. Zana as a Turkish citizen and member of Parliament is under the full protection of the security forces which function under the authority of a democratically established government."[17]

Yet just six months later, on 4 September 1993, Mehmet Sincar, DEP member of parliament for Mardin, was killed in circumstances strongly implicating the security forces. He and Metin Özdemir, Chairman of Batman DEP, were shot dead by three gunmen in broad daylight in the heavily policed city of Batman, southeast Turkey. Other DEP members of parliament who were in Batman at the time of the killings reported that they had been under heavy police surveillance the day before, followed everywhere by at least two vehicles and many plainclothes police officers ostensibly for their "protection." Inexplicably, this unwelcome "protection" disappeared on the morning of 4 September.

In response to an urgent Amnesty International appeal about the killing of Mehmet Sincar, the Turkish Embassy in Madrid replied in December 1993 saying that "investigations by the security forces have resulted in the detention of fifteen suspects. Three of the detainees have confessed to having participated in [the killing of Mehmet Sincar] together with two other persons, all presumed to be members of the radical illegal organization which calls itself Hizbullah." Amnesty International, believing that security forces were colluding with and protecting Hizbullah assassins, was keen to monitor the progress of trials against alleged Hizbullah members and repeatedly requested information from the Justice Ministry about the progress of this and other Hizbullah trials. The Justice Minister did not reply to such requests. But in 1995 a report issued by the IPU[18] revealed how the investigation of Mehmet Sincar's killing, presented by the Turkish Embassy in Madrid as a wrapped up case, actually concluded. All the accused had been acquitted for lack of evidence and released in November 1994.

1. The PKK is an illegal armed organization which began armed attacks on Turkish security forces in August 1984. Since then the conflict, mainly in the rugged rural areas of the six southeastern provinces under state of emergency legislation, has claimed an estimated 27,000 lives. The PKK has been responsible for gross human rights abuses, including the killing of prisoners and civilians.
2. Decision No. 40/1995.
3. Kurdish ethnicity is by no means a disqualification from political or parliamentary activity. More than 100 members of the 550–strong Parliament are said to be of Kurdish origin.
4. In the indictment it was stated that these were the colours of the PKK flag. In fact, the PKK flag is yellow and red only. Red, yellow and green were the colours of the flag of a Kurdish political entity popularly known as "the Mahabad Republic" which existed in Iran from 1946–47. The Court of Appeal ruled that the deputies' wearing of such colours could not be considered an offence since the act occurred within the parliament building and was therefore protected by parliamentary privilege.
5. The minutes of the session noted only that Leyla Zana spoke "in an incomprehensible dialect."
6. The move to lift parliamentary immunity was to some extent triggered by a statement by Hatip Dicle which provoked great public indignation following the deaths of five military students when a bomb planted by the PKK exploded at Tuzla railway station, Istanbul on 12 February 1994. In the indictment it states that Hatip Dicle told *Sabah* [Morning] journalist Guneri Civaoglu: "These students are innocent. But it is natural that in war, innocents are going to be killed if they are military targets. They were wearing military uniforms. Those wearing military uniforms are targets, aren't they? According to the Geneva Convention, military targets may be hit. Civilian targets may not be hit." This was published on 17 February 1994 in *Sabah* under the headline: "DEP's Dicle says PKK's Tuzla attack is normal."
   In an interview with journalist Mehmet Ali Birand broadcast on Show TV on 19 December 1994, Hatip Dicle gave his account of this report: "A few days before the incident, the Chief of General Staff had made a statement [that there is] a war. If there is a war—and this is a military authority; therefore, its assessments are important to me—then the warring sides always try to hit one another's military targets. That is the logic behind war. It is blind logic. It consists of targeting any soldier, anyone in uniform. I did not condone the situation but merely depicted it."
7. *Turkish Daily News*, 23 February 1994.
8. CL/159/11(a)–R.1

9. Four other parliamentary deputies—Ahmet Türk, Sedat Yurttas, Sirri Sakik and Mahmut Alinak—were also indicted and convicted of lesser crimes. At the time of writing this report, none were in custody. For the sake of simplicity, this report deals exclusively with the four former DEP deputies currently serving long sentences.

10. A large number of Sedat Bucak's clan are village guards, armed and paid by the government to fight the PKK. The Turkish press described his following of thousands of village guards as "a private army."

11. The full text of the letter is included in Leyla Zana, *Écrits de Prison*, pp. 31–36, pub. Des Femmes, Paris, November 1995.

12. Handyside v United Kingdom, Judgment of 24 September 1976

13. Mehdi Zana was not able to accept the prize earlier because he himself was serving a one-and-a-half year sentence for statements he had made at the European Parliament about the human rights situation in southeast Turkey.

14. The four can expect to benefit from remission, in which case they will serve eleven years and three months' imprisonment.

15. Case reported in the *Turkish Daily News*, 1 March 1994. Abdullah Kaya had also received death threats.

16. Lawyers and politicians of a visiting British human rights delegation were standing a few metres away as this conversation took place. They did not hear what was said, but reported noticing that the governor of Bismil, who was also present, looked visibly shaken at the gendarmerie commander's words.

17. Letter to Mr. Jim O'Keeffe TD.

18. DH/69/95/MISTUR/R.1, p20—AI Index: EUR 44/85/97.

Amnesty International
1 Easton Street
London WC1X 8DJ
United Kingdom

Appendix-B

U.S. Congressional Appeal on Behalf of Leyla Zana

In November 1997, a bipartisan appeal by the U.S. Congress was forwarded to President Bill Clinton asking for his intervention on behalf of Leyla Zana. The letter of appeal, that was initiated by Rep. Elizabeth Furse (D-OR), Rep. John Edward Porter (R-IL), Rep. Esteban Torres (D-CA), and Rep. Frank R. Wolf (R-VA) was endorsed by 153 members of the U.S. Congress. Congresswoman Furse was the first to raise Leyla Zana's case before Congress in a speech she gave on the House floor in 1994. Subsequently, numerous speeches and appeals have been recorded in the Congress by both Democratic and Republican members, calling for the immediate release of Leyla Zana and other Kurdish Parliamentarians imprisoned in Turkey.

Following are the text of Congressional letter to President Clinton, the President's response, and Leyla Zana's letter of appreciation to the four members of U.S. House of Representatives, respectively.

The Honorable William J. Clinton
The President
The White House
Washington, DC 20500-0005

Dear Mr. President:

We write to draw your attention to the tragic situation of Leyla Zana, the first Kurdish woman ever elected to the Turkish parliament. Mrs. Zana, the mother of two children, was chosen to represent the Kurdish city of Diyarbakir by an overwhelming margin in October of 1991. She was arrested by Turkish authorities on March 2, 1994, in the Parliament building and subsequently prosecuted for what Turkish authorities have labeled "separatist speech," stemming from the exercise of her right to free speech in the defense of the rights of Kurdish people. She was sentenced to fifteen years in prison in December 1994. She remains imprisoned in Ankara today.

One of the charges against Mrs. Zana was her 1993 appearance, here in Washington, before the Helsinki Commission of the United States Congress. We find it outrageous that although she was invited to participate at the request of Members of Congress, her participation was one of the activities that led to her imprisonment.

Mrs. Zana's pursuit of democratic change through nonviolence was honored by the European Parliament which unanimously awarded her the 1995 Sakharov Peace Prize. In addition, Amnesty International and Human Rights Watch have raised concern about her case. Mr. President, Turkey is an important partner of the United States, a NATO member, and a major recipient of our foreign aid, but its abuse of its Kurdish citizens and their legitimately elected representatives is unacceptable. Mrs. Zana's majority Kurdish constituency gave her the mandate to represent them, but the government of Turkey has made an unconscionable effort to stop her. Her voice should not be silenced. This is just one of many cases in which the Turkish government has used the power of the state to abuse people based on their political beliefs.

We ask that you and your administration raise Mrs. Zana's case with the Turkish authorities at the highest level and seek her immediate and unconditional release, so that we may once again welcome her to our shores.

[signed by 153 Members of US Congress]
October 30, 1997

Congress of the United States
Washington, DC 20515

Dear [Member of Congress]:

I received your letter concerning the imprisonment of former Turkish parliamentarian Leyla Zana. I understand your concern that her 1993 appearance before the Commission on Security and Cooperation in Europe of the United States may have helped lead to her imprisonment. We understand that Ms. Zana's comments in Washington were reflected in the overall charges against her, but did not form the primary basis for her conviction.

I assure you that U.S. officials in Ankara and Washington have followed this case closely since it first arose, and have repeatedly stressed to the Government of Turkey the need for due process, respect for human rights, and proper treatment of the accused. Since Ms. Zana's imprisonment, Assistant Secretary of State for Democracy, Human Rights and Labor, John Shattuck and other State Department and Embassy officials have met Ms. Zana in prison.

Ms. Zana's case is being appealed under Council of Europe's Convention on Human Rights through the European Court of Human Rights in Strasbourg. On October 24, 1997, the European Commission of Human Rights (Council of Europe) accepted the application brought by Ms. Zana and her fellow imprisoned former Members of Parliament. We anticipate the Commission will make a determination in the coming weeks. Turkey has publicly confirmed its acceptance of the European Court of Human Rights' judgments, and we expect that to continue to be the case.

The State Department and the U.S. Embassy in Ankara will continue to follow this case. They will also pursue discussion of overall legal reform with the Government of Turkey, an issue that Secretary Albright and I will raise during the December 19 visit of Turkish Prime Minister Yilmaz.
Sincerely,

[Signed, Bill Clinton]

November 20, 1997

October 6, 1997
Ankara Closed Prison

The Honorable Elizabeth Furse
The Honorable John Edward Porter
The Honorable Esteban Torres
The Honorable Frank R. Wolf
United States House of Representatives
Washington, DC 20515

Dear Friends,

With some excitement and great appreciation, I have just found out about the effort you have undertaken on my behalf in the United States Congress. For years now, the Kurdish people have been struggling against great oppression to regain their dignity and identity. Like the other peoples of the world, they too would like to have the freedom to speak their language and to carry on with their traditions. They long to express their political identity.

In Turkey alone, there are some 15 to 20 million Kurds, a figure admitted by the Turkish officials, and yet the democratic aspirations of this constituency have met with blood and tears. Unfortunately, this state of affairs continues to this day. This way of thinking has plunged Turkey into a war that is now fourteen years old. The cease-fire efforts on the part of the Kurds to pave the way for dialogue and peace to this day have gone unnoticed. To this end, I view my imprisonment as synonymous with the freedom of my own people, and I consider your efforts to discuss it in the halls of your Congress very important. I am touched by your spirit of generosity.

Neither my people nor I can ever forget your efforts; we will always remember the gesture with respect.

Your initiative, while uplifting our morale, is also of the utmost importance to the democratic forces in Turkey, the peace activists, the scientists, writers, artists, and the politicians who favor reform. They feel validated and stronger.

On behalf of my fellow imprisoned parliamentarians as well, please accept my warmest greetings and gratitude.

With kindest regards,

Leyla Zana
Member of Parliament

A Bibliography
for Further Reading

Adamson, David. *The Kurdish War*. London: George Allen & Unwin Ltd., 1964.

Ahmed, K.K. *Kurdistan During the First World War*. London: Saqui Books, 1994.

Aydin, Zulkuf. *Underdevelopment and Rural Structures in Southeastern Turkey: The Household Economy in Gisgis and Kalhana*. London: Ithica Press, The Centre for Middle Eastern and Islamic Studies, University of Durham, 1986.

Barkey, Henri J., and Fuller, Graham E. *Turkey's Kurdish Question*. Lanham, MD: Rowman & Littlefield Publishers, 1997.

Bruni, Mary A. and Bruni, Maryann Smothers. *Journey Through Kurdistan*. Dalas: University of Texas Press, 1997.

Bulloch, J., and Morris, H. *No Friends but the Mountains, The Tragic History of the Kurds*. London: Penguin Books, 1992.

Capoglu, Gokhan. *Overcoming the Political Stalemate in Turkey*. Ankara: Strategic Research Foundation, 1995.

Ciment, James. *The Kurds: State and Minority in Turkey, Iraq and Iran (Conflict and Crisis in the Post-Cold War World)*. Lexington: The University Press of Kentucky, 1996.

Chaliand, Gerard (ed.). *A People without a Country: The Kurds and Kurdistan*. Translated by Michael Pallis. London: Zed Press, 1982, and New York: Olive Branch, 1993.

_____. *The Kurdish Tragedy*. Black, Philip (Trans). London & New Jersey: Zed Books, 1994.

Cook, Helena. *The Safe Haven in Northern Iraq: International Responsibility for Iraqi Kurdistan*. London: Human Rights Centre, University of Essex, 1995.

Driver, G.R. *Kurds and Kurdistan*. Mount Carmel, 1919.

Edmonds, C.J. *Kurds, Turks, and Arabs: Politics, Travel and Research in Northern Iraq, 1919–1925*. London, 1957.

Fromkin, David. *A Peace to End All Peace: The Fall of the Ottoman Empire and the Creation of the Modern Middle East*. New York: Henry Holt & Co., 1989.

Gemalmaz, Mehmet Semih. *The Institutionalization Process of the "Turkish Type of Democracy": A Politico-Juridical Analysis of Human Rights*. Istanbul: Amac Yayincilik, 1989.

Ghareeb, E. *The Kurdish Question in Iraq*. Syracuse: University Press, 1981.

Ghassemlou, Abdul Rahman. "Kurdistan and the Kurds" in *A People Without a Country*. New York: Olive Branch Press, 1993.

Gunter, Michael M. *The Kurds and the Future of Turkey*. New York: St. Martin's Press, 1997.

_____. *The Kurds in Turkey*. Boulder, CO: Westview Press, 1990.

_____. *The Kurds of Iraq: Tragedy and Hope*. New York: St. Martin's Press, 1992.

Hassanpour, Amir. *Nationalism and Language in Kurdistan, 1918–85*. San Francisco: Mellen Research University Press, 1992.

Imset, Ismet G. *The PKK: A Report on Separatist Violence in Turkey, 1973–92*. Ankara: Turkish Daily News Publications, 1992.

Izady, Mehrdad R. *The Kurds: A Concise Handbook*. Washington and London: Craen Russak & Co., 1992.

Jawad, S. *Iraq and the Kurdish Question 1958–70*. London: Ithaca, 1981.

Kashi, Ed. (Photographer). *When the Borders Bleed: The Struggle of the Kurds*. New York: Pantheon Books, 1994.

Kinnane, Derk. *The Kurds and Kurdistan*. London & New York: Oxford University Press, 1964.

Kirisci, Kemal and Winrow, Gareth M. *The Kurdish Question and Turkey: An Example of a Trans-State Ethnic Conflict*. England: Frank Cass & CO., 1997.

Kreyenbroek, Philip G.(ed.) and Allison, Christine (ed.). *Kurdish Culture and Identity* London & New Jersey: Zed Books, 1996.

Kreyenbroek, Ph. and Sperl, S. *The Kurds: A Contemporary Overview*. London and New York: Routledge, 1992.

Laizer, Sheri. *Into Kurdistan: Frontiers Under Fire*. London & New Jersey: Zed Books, 1992

_____. *Martyrs, Traitors and Patriots: Kurdistan after the Gulf War*. London and New Jersey: Zed Books, 1996.

Mayall, Simon V. *Turkey: Thwarted Ambition*. Washington, DC: National Defense University, Institute for National Strategic Studies, 1997.

McDowall, David. *A Modern History of the Kurds Vol 1*. London: I.B. Tauris, 1996.

_____. *The Kurds, A Nation Denied*. London: Minority Rights Publications, 1992.

Meho, Lokman I. (Compiler). *The Kurds and Kurdistan: A Selective and Annotated Bibliography (Bibliographies and Indexes in World History, No. 46)*. Westport, CT: Greenwood Publ. Group, 1997.

Meiselas, Susan. *Kurdistan: In the Shadow of History*. New York: Random House, 1997.

Nezan, Kendal. "The Kurds Under the Ottoman Empire" in *A People Without a Country*. New York: Olive Branch Press, 1993.

O'Ballance, Edgar. *The Kurdish Struggle, 1920–94*. New York: St. Martin's Press, 1996.

Olson, Robert. "The Creation of a Kurdish State in the 1990s?" *Journal of South Asian & Middle Eastern Studies*. Summer 1992, Vol. 15, No. 4.

_____. *The Emergence of Kurdish Nationalism and the Sheikh Said Rebellion, 1880–1925*. Austin: University of Texas Press, 1989.

Olson, Robert (ed.). *The Kurdish Nationalist Movement in the 1990s: Its Impact on Turkey and the Middle East*. Lexington: The University Press of Kentucky, 1996.

Pelletiere, Stephen C. *The Kurds: An Unstable Element in the Gulf*. Boulder, CO: Waterview Press, 1984.

Randal, Jonathan C. *After Such Knowledge, What Forgiveness? My Encounters with Kurdistan*. New York: Farrar, Straus and Grioux, 1997.

Rugman, J., and Hutchings, R. *Atatürk's Children: Turkey and the Kurds*. London and New York: Cassell, 1996.

Safrastian, Arshak. *Kurds and Kurdistan*. London, 1948.

Sauar, Erik. *Turkey's Struggle with Democracy and Kurds—An Authority, Information and Terrorism Perspective*. Norway: Norwegian University of Science and Technology, Department of Social Anthropology, 1996.

Soane, E.B. *To Mesopotamia and Kurdistan in Disguise*. London: John Murray, 1912.

Scmidt, Dana Adams. *Journey among Brave Men*. Foreword by Justice William O. Douglas. Boston & Toronto: Little, Brown and Company, 1964.

White, Paul (ed.). *The Kurds in World Politics: Papers and Resources for Studying the Kurds.* Malvern, Victoria, Australia: CSAME Special Issues Series, Deakin University, 1995.

Van Bruinessen, Martin. *Agha, Sheikh and State: The Social and Political Structures of Kurdistan.* London & New Jersey: Zed Books, 1992.

_____. "Kurdish Society, Ethnicity, Nationalism and Refugee Problems" in P.G. Kreyenbroek and S. Sperl (eds.), *The Kurds: A Contemporary Overview.* London: Routledge, 1992.

Yassin, Borhanedin A., *Vision or Reality? The Kurds in the Policy of the Great Powers, 1941–1947.* Lund: Lund University Press, Studies in International History, 1995.

Yilmaz, Bahri. *Challenges to Turkey: The New Role of Turkey in International Politics since the Dissolution of the Soviet Union.* New York: St. Martin's Press, 1997.

Publications by Human Rights Groups and Organizations:

A number of International human rights groups and organizations publish newsletters, special reports, and studies on human rights violations in Turkey and other countries. These reports and publications are available from the organizations such as Amnesty International, Human Rights Watch/Helsinki, Human Rights Watch/Middle East, Initiative for Human Rights in Kurdistan, Human Rights Foundation of Turkey, Kurdish Institute of Paris, Kurdish Information Network, and Washington Kurdish Institute.

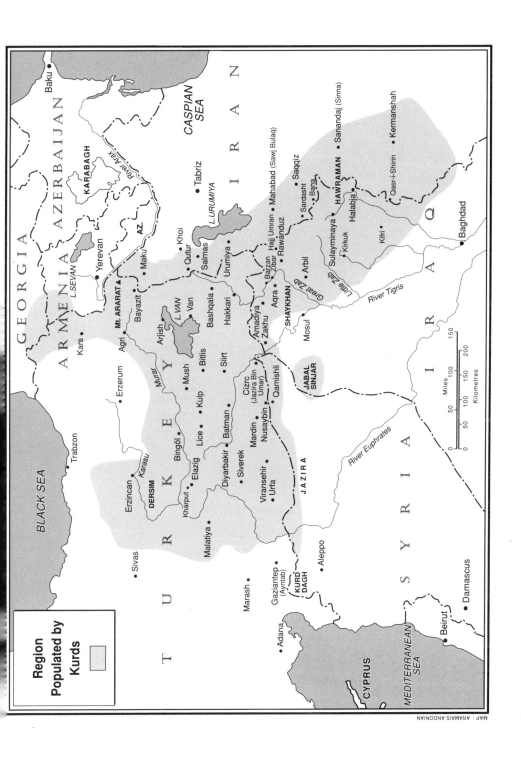

Region Populated by Kurds

BLACK SEA

GEORGIA

ARMENIA

AZERBAIJAN

KARABAGH

AZ.

Baku

River Araxes

CASPIAN SEA

I R A N

L.SEVAN

Yerevan

Kars

Mt. ARARAT

Bayazit

Maku

Khoi

Qutur

Salmas

Urumiya

Tabriz

L.URUMIYA

Haji Umran

Rawanduz

Zibar

Barzan

Mahabad (Sawj Bulaq)

Sardasht

Bana

Saqqiz

Sanandaj (Sinna)

HAWRAMAN

Kermanshah

Qasr-i-Shirin

Baghdad

Trabzon

Erzerum

Erzincan

Sivas

DERSIM

Murat

Karasu

Agri

Arjish

L.VAN

Van

Bashqala

Hakkari

Amadiya

Zakhu

Aqra

Arbil

Great Zab

Little Zab

SHAYKHAN

Mosul

River Tigris

Sulaymaniya

Kirkuk

Kifri

Halabja

I R A Q

Mush

Bitlis

Siirt

Bingöl

Kulp

Lice

Batman

Diyarbakir

Siverek

Mardin

Nusaybin

Viranşehir

Urfa

Cizre (Jazira Bin Umar)

Qamishli

JABAL SINJAR

JAZIRA

T U R K E Y

Kharput

Elazig

Malatiya

Marash

Gaziantep (Ayntab)

KURD DAGH

Aleppo

Adana

S Y R I A

River Euphrates

CYPRUS

MEDITERRANEAN SEA

Beirut

Damascus

Miles

Kilometres

0 50 100 150 200

0 50 100 150